ESSENTIALS OF MANAGING STRESS DURING TIMES OF PANDEMIC

A PRIMER

ESSENTIALS OF MANAGING STRESS DURING TIMES OF PANDEMIC

A PRIMER

BRIAN LUKE SEAWARD

JONES & BARTLETT
LEARNING

World Headquarters
Jones & Bartlett Learning
5 Wall Street
Burlington, MA 01803
978-443-5000
info@jblearning.com
www.jblearning.com

Jones & Bartlett Learning books and products are available through most bookstores and online booksellers. To contact Jones & Bartlett Learning directly, call 800-832-0034, fax 978-443-8000, or visit our website, www.jblearning.com.

34910-8

Production Credits

VP, Product Development: Christine Emerton
Director of Product Management: Cathy Esperti
Product Manager: Whitney Fekete
Content Strategist: Ashley Malone
Content Coordinator: Elena Sorrentino
Project Manager: Kristen Rogers
Project Specialist: Meghan McDonagh
Senior Digital Project Specialist: Angela Dooley
Director of Marketing: Andrea DeFronzo
Content Services Manager: Colleen Lamy
VP, Manufacturing and Inventory Control: Therese Connell
Composition: SPi Global
Project Management: SPi Global
Cover Design: Briana Yates
Text Design: Briana Yates
Senior Media Development Editor: Troy Liston
Rights Specialist: Benjamin Roy
Cover Image (Title Page, Part Opener, Chapter Opener): © Inspiration Unlimited. Used with permission.
Printing and Binding: McNaughton & Gunn

Library of Congress Cataloging-in-Publication Data

Names: Seaward, Brian Luke, author.
Title: Essentials of managing stress during times of pandemic : a primer / Brian Luke Seaward.
Description: First edition. | Burlington, Massachusetts : Jones & Bartlett Learning, [2022] | Includes bibliographical references and index.
Identifiers: LCCN 2020056037 | ISBN 9781284230543 (paperback)
Subjects: LCSH: Stress management. | Stress (Psychology) | Mind and body.
Classification: LCC RA785 .S432955 2022 | DDC 155.9/042--dc23
LC record available at https://lccn.loc.gov/2020056037

6048

Printed in the United States of America
25 24 23 22 21   10 9 8 7 6 5 4 3 2 1

This book is dedicated to the frontline nurses and healthcare professionals worldwide who care for countless sick and dying people. Selfless, they put others first while risking their own lives to administer care. A heartfelt thanks of deep gratitude.

Brief Contents

Contents

PART I What Is Stress?   1

PART II Effective Coping Skills   61

PART III Stress Relief Techniques 81

PART IV Ten Quick Tips for Staying Grounded 103

Preface

A number of words and expressions have repeatedly filled the airwaves and personal conversations regarding the current coronavirus pandemic (COVID-19): *crisis, calamity, anger, stress, unprecedented, lives-turned-upside-down, anxiety, overwhelming, exhausted, sadness, grief, difficulty, pandemic fatigue, the new normal,* and *angst,* just to name some. Conversely, another word that has been used with equal measure is *resiliency,* and for good reason: we human beings are quite resilient by nature. This much is certain: we will get through this chapter of humanity, just as we have for other national and global difficulties. We can take either of two paths: go gracefully or emerge as victims. The choice is ours and, to be honest, there really is no choice—nobody wants to be a victim.

Resiliency means to bounce back, to recover, to thrive in the face of adversity. This is the time to pick ourselves up, dust ourselves off, hold our heads high, and carry on. Yet resiliency doesn't happen all by itself. We must engage in the process. We must persist. We must adapt. There really is no other way.

This pandemic has certainly been a test in patience, kindness, willpower, and inner strength. The challenges and lessons learned have been many. A few notable things have been observed by many already: (1) people are reading more books (not eBooks but actual books—with covers); (2) board games and jigsaw puzzles have made a resurgence in small-group activities at home; and (3) people have rediscovered the great outdoors, with increased bike sales, fishing license applications, and bird feeder purchases. In fact, interest in birding has increased tenfold since the start of the pandemic as people developed a deep-seated fascination with backyard wildlife.

At some point, life will return to a sense of normalcy. Before that happens, however, we have a choice and a say in how that will look. In these profound words of David Hollis, "In the rush to return to normal, use this time to consider which parts of normal are worth rushing back to." The words and wisdom found in this book offer many insights and proven strategies to help keep you above the fray. May we all use this time wisely. May we all emerge from this gracefully.

Brian Luke Seaward, PhD
The Paramount Wellness Institute
Boulder, Colorado

Introduction

Keeping Above the Fray

An Introduction

How does one navigate one's life in extremely difficult times? That question has been asked by countless people for millennia. Typically, we ask for help. We talk to friends and family. We contemplate our options. We model and copy efforts and behaviors of others who have succeeded, and we even think up new options and try new strategies ourselves. We read books that contain insights and wisdom, which together act like both map and compass to help us chart a course for smoother waters. This is one such book.

This text was designed as a quick read to remind you of what you already know, as well as to introduce a few new concepts that serve as stepping stones for you to leap over troubled waters in these challenging times and, ultimately, to secure firm footing on solid ground. Pandemic or no pandemic, basic stress management is common sense, but during troubled times such as these, common sense is not always common. As such, a review of common wisdom never hurts. In fact, it's essential.

As we all know, stress comes in ripples. Lately, we have learned it even comes in tsunamis. The year 2020 was a tsunami. Stress is indeed part of the human landscape, yet with each passing year, new stressors grab our attention. Before the pandemic washed ashore, two of the biggest health issues—specifically stress-related issues observed by psychologists and health educators—were alienation and isolation. Since the pandemic, where lockdowns and social isolation were mandated to flatten the curves, alienation and isolation have increased dramatically. With these mandates, experts have seen a dramatic increase in mental health issues, suicide, self-medication, alcoholism, and even binge watching, addictive social media postings, nonstop video gaming, and scores of behaviors that fall under the heading of screen addictions.

Yet with all of these challenges in the crazy year of 2020 and beyond, we are also given a chance to pause and plan a reset so that we can avoid further calamities and crises. This book can help.

This book contains four sections—Part I: What Is Stress?; Part II: Effective Coping Skills; Part III: Stress Relief Techniques; and Part IV: Ten Quick Tips for Staying Grounded.

Part I: What Is Stress? This is a quick review of some basics about the nature of stress; the psychology of stress: anger (fight) and fear (flight); and the mind-body connection and how emotional stress affects the physical body.

Part II: Effective Coping Skills. Coping skills fall into two categories: effective and noneffective. Noneffective coping skills fall under the category of avoidance. Ultimately, they do not help to resolve stress. In fact, they tend to perpetuate it. The chapters in this section highlight two popular and effective coping skills: adopting a positive mind-set (also known as reframing) and creative problem solving.

Part III: Stress Relief Techniques. There are hundreds of relaxation techniques, but for starters nutrition (eating for a healthy immune system) and physical exercise are two of the most important.

Part IV: Ten Quick Tips. These strategies offer the reader some easily accessible ideas to create a personal plan for optimal resiliency as well as some human interest stories (Stress with a Human Face) to inspire the reader.

Included in this book are several exercises and questionnaires to help you put into play your own resiliency action plan. Together, all of the wisdom and insights offer you an abundance of ageless wisdom and timeless advice to help you navigate your life gracefully in these times. What may seem like a short book to supplement your understanding of coping with stress in hard times is really a template for inner peace. Enjoy!

Acknowledgments

This book would never have seen the light of day had it not been for the foresight of Whitney Fekete, who within the first few weeks of the COVID-19 pandemic jumped into action to gather resources and people to make this spinoff of *Essentials of Managing Stress* possible. Thanks, Whitney, for your inspiration and dedication. If one person benefits from reading this book, we shall have made the world a better place.

Many thanks also to Ashley Malone who marshalled all kinds of resources to manifest this book. It's always a pleasure working with you, Ashley, and all the Jones & Bartlett Learning staff.

Resources

ESSENTIALS OF
MANAGING STRESS
DURING TIMES OF
PANDEMIC
A PRIMER

BRIAN LUKE SEAWARD

JONES & BARTLETT
LEARNING

Each book includes access to a dynamic and packed online resource! The Navigate Companion Website provides workbook activities, audio introductions from the author, a relaxation audio, weblinks, and practice exercises.

Relaxation Media and Audio Introductions

In his own words, the author, Brian Luke Seaward, introduces each of the four sections in the book. He provides a summary of each chapter in each section and explains why the information is so important to the understanding and management of stress. This is a great resource for students and instructors!

Workbook

The workbook provides worksheets as printable and writable PDFs for students to apply their knowledge of stress management.

Practice Exercises

Practice exercises provide students with the opportunity to apply what they've learned.

Weblinks

Weblinks provide additional learning materials for students to enjoy while using this text.

PART I

What Is Stress?

CHAPTER 1

The Nature of Stress

KEY TERMS

Acute stress
Alarm reaction
Auto-immune diseases
Bioecological influence
Chronic stress
Circadian rhythms
Cortisol
Daily life hassles
Distress
Effective coping skills
Effective relaxation techniques
Eustress
Fight-or-flight response
Freeze response
General adaptation syndrome (GAS)
Holistic medicine
Homeostasis
Infradian rhythms
Life change units (LCUS)
Mechanistic model

Neuropeptides
Neustress
Psychointrapersonal influences
Richard Lazarus
Seasonal affective disorder
  (SAD)
Sleep hygiene
Social influences
Social Readjustment Rating Scale
  (SRRS)
Stage of exhaustion
Stage of resistance
Stressor
Stress reaction
Stress response
Technostress
Tend and befriend
Ultradian rhythms
Walter Cannon
Yerkes-Dodson principle

Are you stressed? If the answer is yes, then consider yourself to be in good company. Stress before the coronavirus pandemic of 2020 was noted to be at the highest level in decades, an all-too-common behavioral trend. According to a Gallup poll, in 2019 Americans already had reported the highest stress levels (anger and anxiety) in a decade, distinguishing them as the most stressed people in the world. The coronavirus (COVID-19) epidemic, which started in the late winter of 2020, has only made matters worse, with the United States surpassing China, Italy, India, and Brazil in the number of those infected. Deaths due to the pandemic are equally disturbing. Moreover, the impact of the pandemic, including on those physically affected by COVID-19 and the panic it produced, has resulted in stress in the forms of anger, anxiety, and exhaustion around the world. Mandated lockdowns, self-isolation, panic buying, massive layoffs, face masks, pandemic fatigue, work furloughs, social distancing, forced immobilization, canceled high school and college graduations, postponed weddings, canceled professional sports events, empty stadiums, closed Broadway productions, closed movie theaters, bare grocery store shelves, online funerals—nearly every aspect of society has been affected by this worldwide pandemic. Boredom, impatience, defiance, frustration, and fear have all surfaced as people continue to try to get by in the face of adversity. The world we were raised in is *not* the world we are living in now.

Several recent Harris and Gallup polls have noted an alarming trend in the psyche of the American public and beyond—to nearly all citizens of the global village. Across the board, without exception, people admit to having an increasing sense of anxiety, frustration, unease, and discontent in nearly every aspect of their lives. These problems include personal finances and long-term debt, domestic terrorism, political disgust, and the sustained impact of environmental disasters. As such, the face of stress can be found just about everywhere. Sadly, episodes of suicides, opioid addiction, school shootings, and personal bankruptcies are now so common that they no longer make the headline news as they once did. Ironically, in a country where the standard of living is considered to be the highest of anywhere in the world, the Centers for Disease Control and Prevention estimates that nearly one-quarter of the U.S. population is reported to be on antidepressants. Estimates also suggest that one in three people suffer from a chronic disease, ranging from cancer and coronary heart disease (CHD) to diabetes, lupus, and rheumatoid arthritis. For a country with one of the highest standards of living, something is very wrong with this picture.

Furthermore, since the start of the pandemic, a blanket of fear has covered much of the United States, if not the world, keeping people in a perpetual, albeit low, state of anxiety. Global problems only seem to intensify our personal stressors. It doesn't make a difference if you're a college student or a CEO of a multinational corporation, where you live, or how much money is in your checking account—stress is the equal opportunity destroyer! But it doesn't have to be this way. Even as personal issues collide with social and planetary problems creating a "perfect storm" of stress, we all have choices—in both our attitude and behaviors. This text will help you connect the dots between mind, body, and spirit to create positive choices that empower you to navigate your life through the turbulent waters of the human journey in the 21st century.

Times of Change and Uncertainty

Today the words *stress* and *change* have become synonymous, and the winds of change are in the air, particularly with the ripples from the Covid pandemic. Changes in the economy, technology, communications, information retrieval, social media, and health care, as well as dramatic changes in the weather, are just some of the gale forces blowing in our collective faces. By and large, the average person doesn't like change (particularly change they cannot control) because change tends to disrupt one's comfort zones. It appears that the "known," no matter how bad, is a safer bet than the unknown. Change, it should be noted, has always been part of the human landscape. However, today the rate of change has become so fast and furious, without an adequate reference point on which to anchor oneself, that stress holds the potential to create a perpetual sense of uneasiness in the hearts and minds of nearly everyone. Yet it doesn't have to be this way. Where there is change, there is opportunity.

At one time, getting married, changing jobs, buying a house, raising children, going back to school, dealing with the death of a friend or close relative, and suffering from a chronic illness were all considered to be major life events that might shake the foundations of anyone's life. Although these major life events can and do play a significant role in personal upheaval, a new crop of social stressors has added to the critical mass of an already volatile existence, throwing things further out of balance. Consider how the following factors directly influence your life: the rapid acceleration of technology (from software upgrades to downloadable apps), the use of (if not addiction to) social media (e.g., Facebook, Instagram, Snapchat, and Twitter), the proliferation of smartphones and Wi-Fi use, an accessible 24/7 society, global economic woes (e.g., gasoline prices, school loans, rent, food prices), global terrorism, carbon footprints, and public health issues from AIDS and West Nile virus to the latest outbreak of contagious *Staphylococcus* infections. Times of change and uncertainty tend to magnify our personal stress. Perhaps the biggest looming concern facing people today is the issue of personal boundaries or lack thereof. The advances of high technology combined with a rapidly changing social structure have eroded personal boundaries. These boundaries include, but are not limited to, home and work, finances, personal privacy, nutritional habits, relationships, and many, many more, all of which add to the critical mass of one's personal stress. Even the ongoing war on terrorism appears to have no boundaries! Ironically, the lack of boundaries combined with factors that promote a fractured society, in which people feel a lack of community and belonging, leads to a greater sense of alienation and isolation, and this also intensifies our personal stress levels. Believe it or not, life wasn't always like this.

The stress phenomenon, as it is referred to today, is quite new with regard to the history of humanity. Barely a household expression when your parents were of your age, use of the word *stress* is now as common as the terms *global warming*, *iPads*, and *smartphones*. In fact, however, stress in terms of physical arousal can be traced back to the Stone Age as a "survival mechanism." But what was once designed as a means of survival is now associated with the development of diseases and illnesses that claim the lives of millions of people worldwide. The American Institute of Stress (www.stress.org) cites the following statistics:

- 43 percent of all adults suffer adverse health effects due to stress.
- 75–90 percent of all visits to primary care physicians are for stress-related complaints or disorders.

Stress has been linked to all the leading causes of death, including heart disease, cancer, lung ailments, accidents, cirrhosis, and suicide. Some health experts speculate that perhaps as much as 70–85 percent of all diseases and illnesses are stress related.

Comprehensive studies conducted by both the American Psychological Association (APA) and the Harvard School of Public Health have provided a host of indicators suggesting that human stress is indeed a health factor to be reckoned with. Prior to 1955, the leading causes of death were the sudden onset of illness by infectious diseases (e.g., polio, rubella, tuberculosis, typhoid, and encephalitis) that in most cases have since been eradicated or brought under control by vaccines and medications. The post–World War II era ushered in the age of high technology, which considerably altered the lifestyles of nearly all peoples of every industrialized nation. The start of the 21st century has seen the influence of high technology on our lifestyles. The introduction of consumer products, such as the washer, dryer, microwave oven, television, DVD player, laptop computer, and smartphone, were cited as luxuries to add more leisure time to the workweek. But as mass production of high-technology items increased, so too did the competitive drive to increase human effort and productivity, which in turn actually decreased leisure time, and thus created a plethora of unhealthy lifestyles, most notably resulting in obesity.

Currently, the leading causes of death are dominated by what are referred to as lifestyle diseases—those diseases whose pathology develops over a period of several years, and perhaps even decades. Whereas infectious diseases are treatable by medication, lifestyle diseases are, for the most part, preventable or correctable by altering the habits and behaviors that contribute to their etiology. Previously, it was suggested that an association existed between stress and disease. Current research, however, suggests that there may indeed be a causal factor involved in several types of diseases, particularly heart disease, obesity, and **auto-immune diseases**. Regardless, it is well understood that the influence of stress weakens the body's physiological systems, thereby rapidly advancing the disease process. The most notorious lifestyle disease, CHD, continues to be one of the leading causes of death in the United States, far exceeding all other causes. The American Heart Association states that one person dies from heart disease every 34 seconds. Although the incidence of CHD has decreased over the past decade, cancer—in all its many types—continues to climb the statistical charts as the second leading cause of death. According to 2012 statistics from the American Cancer Society (www.cancer.org), cancer claims the lives of one out of every four people in the United States. Alarming increases in suicides, child and spouse abuse, self-mutilation, homicides, alcoholism, and drug addiction are additional symptoms of a nation under stress. Today, research shows that people still maintain poor coping skills in the face of the personal, social, and even global changes occurring over the course of their lives.

Originally, the word *stress* was a term used in physics, primarily to describe enough tension or force placed on an object to bend or break it. *Relaxation*, on the other hand, was defined as any nonwork activity done during the evenings or on Sunday afternoons when all the stores were closed. On rare occasions, if one could afford it, relaxation meant a vacation or holiday at some faraway place. Conceptually, relaxation was a value, influenced by several religions and represented as a day of rest.

The word *stress* as applied to the human condition was first made popular by noted physiologist and endocrinologist Hans Selye, who created a name for himself as a leading researcher in this field. In his book *The Stress of Life*, he described his research: to understand the physiological responses to chronic stress and its relationship to disease (dis-ease). Today, the word *stress* is frequently used to describe the level of tension that people feel is placed on their minds and souls by the demands of their jobs, relationships, and responsibilities in their personal lives. Oddly, for some, stress seems to be a status symbol tied to self-esteem.

Despite various economic changes over time, some interesting insights have been observed regarding work and leisure. The average workweek has expanded from 40 to 60 hours. The U.S. Department of Labor and Statistics reports that with more service-related jobs being created, more overtime is needed to meet customer demand. Not only do more people spend more time at work, but they also spend more time driving to and from work (which is not considered work time). Moreover, leisure time at home is often related to work activities, resulting in less time for rest and relaxation. For many, work–life balance has become a myth. Downtime is also compromised. Since 2001, Expedia has conducted the Vacation Deprivation survey, an annual survey about vacations. The 2018 results revealed that one out of every three Americans doesn't use all of his or her vacation time. One in five respondents cited work responsibilities and pressure as the primary reason for canceling a vacation. A new word entered the American lexicon in the summer of 2008—and came into repeated use during the COVID-19 pandemic): the *staycation*, during which people stayed home for vacation due to financial or work constraints. Those who do head for the mountains or beaches for vacation often take their work (in the form of smartphones and laptops) with them—in essence, never really leaving their job. It's no surprise that staying plugged in doesn't give the mind a chance to unwind or the body a chance to relax. By comparison with other countries, Americans take less vacation time than other global citizens (Germans, on average, take 4 to 6 weeks per year). According to Tim MacDonald, general manager of Expedia, "The stress associated with the current economy makes the need for time away from work even more important than ever, and it's unfortunate that one-third of Americans won't use all of their vacation days this year." The "dividend" of high technology has proven to be an illusion for many that has resulted in a stressed lifestyle, which, in turn, creates a significant health deficit.

Definitions of Stress

In contemporary times, the word *stress* has many connotations and definitions based on various perspectives of the human condition. In Eastern philosophies, stress is considered to be an absence of inner peace. In Western culture, stress can be described as a loss of emotional control. Noted healer Serge Kahili King has defined stress as any change experienced by an individual. This definition may be rather general, but it is quite correct. Psychologically speaking, stress as defined by noted researcher Richard Lazarus is a state of anxiety produced when events and responsibilities exceed one's coping abilities. Physiologically speaking, stress is defined as the rate of wear and tear on the body. Selye added to his definition that stress is the nonspecific response of the body to any demand placed upon it to adapt, whether that demand produces pleasure or pain. Selye observed that whether a situation was perceived as good (e.g., a job promotion) or bad (e.g., the loss of a job), the physiological response or arousal was very similar. The body, according to Selye, doesn't know the difference between good and bad stress.

However, with new psychoneuroimmunological data available showing that there are indeed some physiological differences between good and bad stress (e.g., the release of different **neuropeptides**), specialists in the field of **holistic medicine** have expanded Lazarus's and Selye's definitions as follows: Stress is the inability to cope with a perceived (real or imagined) threat to one's mental, physical, emotional, and spiritual well-being, which results in a series of physiological responses and adaptations. The important word to emphasize here is *perceived* (the interpretation), for what might seem to be a threat to one person may not even merit a second thought to another individual. For example, not long ago a raffle was held, with the winning prize being an all-expenses-paid one-week trip for two to a beach resort in Bermuda. Kelly, who won the prize, was ecstatic and already had her bags packed. Her husband, John, was mortified because he hated to fly and he couldn't swim. In his mind this would not be a fun time. In fact, he really wished they hadn't won. Each perceived the same situation in entirely different ways. Moreover, with the wisdom of hindsight, our perceptions often change. Many episodes that at the time seem catastrophic later appear insignificant, as humorously stated by Mark Twain when he commented, "I'm an old man and I have known a great many troubles, but most of them never happened." The holistic definition of stress points out that it is a very complex phenomenon affecting the whole person, not just the physical body, and that it involves a host of factors, some of which may not yet even be recognized by scholars and researchers. As more research is completed, it becomes increasingly evident that the responses to stress add up to more than just physical arousal; yet it is ultimately the body that remains the battlefield for the war games of the mind.

The Stress Response

In 1914, Harvard physiologist **Walter Cannon** first coined the term **fight-or-flight response** to describe the dynamics involved in the body's physiological arousal to survive a threat. In a series of animal studies, Cannon noted that the body prepares itself for one of two modes of immediate action: to attack or fight and defend oneself from the pursuing threat, or to run and escape the ensuing danger. What Cannon observed was the body's reaction to acute stress, what is now commonly called the **stress reaction**. Additional observations suggested that the fight response was triggered by anger or aggression and was usually employed to defend territorial boundaries or attack aggressors equal or smaller in size. The fight response required physiological preparations that would recruit power and strength for a short duration, or what is now described as short but intense anaerobic work. Conversely, the flight response, he thought, was induced by fear. It was designed to fuel the body to endure prolonged movement such as running away from lions and bears. In many cases, however, it included not only fleeing but also hiding or withdrawal. (A variation on the flight response is the **freeze response**, often noted with posttraumatic stress disorder (PTSD), where a person simply freezes, like a deer staring into a vehicle's headlights.) The human body, in all its metabolic splendor, actually prepares itself to do both (fight and flight) at the same time. In terms of evolution, it appears that this dynamic was so advantageous to survival that it developed in nearly all mammalian species, including humans. (Some experts now suggest, however, that our bodies have not adapted to the stress-induced lifestyles of the 21st century.)

In simple terms, there are four stages of the fight-or-flight response:

- *Stage 1*: Stimuli from one or more of the five senses are sent to the brain (e.g., a scream, the smell of fire, the taste of poison, a passing truck in your lane).
- *Stage 2*: The brain deciphers the stimulus as either a threat or a nonthreat. If the stimulus is not regarded as a threat, this is the end of the response (e.g., the scream came from the television). If, however, the response is decoded as a real threat, the brain then activates the nervous and endocrine systems to quickly prepare for defense and/or escape.
- *Stage 3*: The body stays activated, aroused, or keyed up until the threat is over.
- *Stage 4*: The body returns to **homeostasis**, a state of physiological calm, once the threat is gone.

It is hypothesized that the fight-or-flight response developed primarily against those threats of a physical nature that jeopardized the survival of the individual. Although clear physical threats still exist today, including possible terrorism, they are nowhere near as prevalent as those threats perceived by the mind and, more specifically, the ego. In a theory put forward by a disciple of Selye, A. T. W., and repeated by Robert Sapolsky, it is suggested that, in effect, the fight-or-flight response is an antiquated mechanism that has not kept evolutionary pace with the development of the human mind. Consequently, the **stress response** becomes activated in all types of threats, not just physical intimidations. The physiological repercussions can, and do, prove fatal. The body enters a state of physical readiness when you are about to receive your final exam grades or walk into an important meeting late, just as it does when you sense someone is following you late at night in an unlit parking lot. Moreover, this same stress response kicks in, to the same degree and intensity, even when the threat is wholly imaginary, in reaction to everything from monsters hiding under your bed when you were four years old, to the unsubstantiated idea that your boss doesn't like you anymore and is out to get you.

Cannon noted the activation of several physiological mechanisms in this fight-or-flight response, affecting nearly every physiological system in the body, for the preparation of movement and energy production. These are just a few of the reactions:

- Increased heart rate to pump oxygenated blood to working muscles
- Increased blood pressure to deliver blood to working muscles
- Increased ventilation to supply working muscles with oxygen for energy metabolism
- Vasodilation of arteries to the body's periphery (arms and legs) with the greatest muscle mass
- Increased serum glucose for metabolic processes during muscle contractions
- Increased free-fatty-acid mobilization as an energy source for prolonged activity (e.g., running)
- Increased blood coagulation and decreased clotting time in the event of bleeding
- Increased muscular strength
- Decreased gastric movement and abdominal blood flow to allow blood to go to working muscles
- Increased perspiration to cool core body temperature

Unfortunately, the metabolic and physiological changes that are deemed essential for human movement in the event of attack, pursuit, or challenge are quite ineffective when dealing with events or situations that threaten the ego, such as receiving a parking ticket or standing in a long line at the grocery store, yet the body responds identically to all types of perceived threats.

Tend and Befriend

Do women respond differently to stress than men do? The answer may seem obvious. Generally speaking, men are prone to act more hostile, whereas women have a proclivity to be more nurturing. Yet until recently every source on stress addressed the fight-or-flight response as if it were the only human default response. It was the work of Shelley Taylor and colleagues that filled in the missing piece with regard to the female response to stress. Curious about why only men were studied to formulate the basis for the fight-or-flight response, Taylor hypothesized that the stress response needed to be reexamined, this time including astute observations of the female gender. In 2000, Taylor and colleagues proposed a new theory for the female stress response that they termed **tend and befriend**. Although both men and women have a built-in dynamic for surviving physical danger, women also have an inherent nurturing response for their offspring as well as a means to befriend others. This in turn creates a strong social support system that is an invaluable coping technique. Taylor suggests that the female response to stress is hardwired into the DNA and revealed through a combination of brain chemistry and hormones. The biological basis for tend and befriend appears to be the hormone oxytocin, now regarded as the "trusting hormone" or the "social affiliation hormone." Although oxytocin is found in both women and, to a lesser degree, in men, estrogen is known to enhance the effects of oxytocin in the brain. Generational social factors may support the tend-and-befriend behavior pattern as well.

Not only do men and women have differences in their stress physiology, but there appear to be gender-specific behaviors for discussing and solving problems as well. Whereas men tend to think their way through by looking for solutions to problems, women like to talk about problems. Women bond quickly by sharing confidences. However, although talking may be beneficial, researchers note that merely talking about stressors tends to perpetuate rather than solve one's stressors. Researchers refer to stress-based conversations as "co-rumination." Although talking may strengthen female friendships, it is also known to increase anxiety and depression if solutions aren't introduced quickly. Experts such as Laura Sessions Stepp warn against "unhealthy rumination" and the emotional contagion that results from it.

It is fair to say that the concepts of survival are complex and perhaps not so neatly packaged by hormones or gender. Women are known to backstab their "friends" and regrettably, on occasion, to ditch their newborn babies in dumpsters and run away. Conversely, some men choose peace over violence (Mahatma Gandhi and Martin Luther King, Jr., come to mind), and when times get tough, men are known to bond together over a beer or game of golf.

Types of Stress

To the disbelief of some, not all stress is bad for you. In fact, many people believe that humans need some degree of stress to stay healthy. The human body craves homeostasis, or physiological calm, yet it also requires physiological arousal to ensure the optimal functioning of several organs, including the heart and musculoskeletal system. How can stress be good? When stress serves as positive motivation, it is considered beneficial. Beyond this optimal point, stress of any kind does more harm than good.

Actually, there are three kinds of stress: eustress, neustress, and distress. **Eustress** is good stress and arises in any situation or circumstance that a person finds motivating or inspiring. Falling in love might be an example of eustress; meeting a movie star or professional athlete may also be a type of eustress. Usually, situations that are classified as eustress are enjoyable and for this reason are not considered to be a threat. **Neustress** describes sensory stimuli that have no consequential effect; it is considered neither good nor bad. News of an earthquake in a remote corner of the world might fall into this category. The third type of stress, **distress**, is considered bad and often is referred to simply as stress. There are two kinds of distress: **acute stress**, which surfaces, is quite intense, and disappears quickly, and **chronic stress**, which may not appear quite so intense, yet seems to linger for prolonged periods (e.g., hours, days, weeks, or months).

An example of acute stress is the following: You are casually driving down the highway, the wind from the open sunroof is blowing through your hair, and you feel pretty good about life. With a quick glance in your rearview mirror, you see flashing blue lights. Yikes! So you slow down and pull over. The police car pulls up behind you. Your heart is racing, your voice becomes scratchy, and your palms are sweating as you try to retrieve license and registration from your wallet while rolling your window down at the same time. When the officer asks you why you were speeding you can barely speak; your voice is three octaves higher than usual. After the officer runs a check on your car and license, he only gives you a warning for speeding. Whew! He gets back in his car and leaves. You give him time to get out of sight, start your engine, and signal to get back onto the highway. Within minutes your heart is calm, your palms dry, and you start singing to the song on the radio. The threat is over. The intensity of the acute stress may seem cataclysmic, but it is very short-lived.

Chronic stressors, on the other hand, are not as intense but their duration is unbearably long. Examples might include the following: being stuck for a whole semester with "the roommate from hell," a credit card bill that only seems to grow despite monthly payments, a boss who makes your job seem worse than that of a galley slave, living in a city you cannot tolerate, or maintaining a relationship with a girlfriend, boyfriend, husband, or wife that seems bad to stay in but worse to leave. For this reason, chronic stressors are thought to be the real villains. According to the American Institute of Stress (AIS), it is chronic stress that is associated with disease because the body is perpetually aroused for danger.

A concept called the **Yerkes-Dodson principle**, which is applied to athletic performance, lends itself quite nicely to explaining the relationship among eustress, distress, and health. As can be seen in **Figure 1.1**, when stress increases, moving

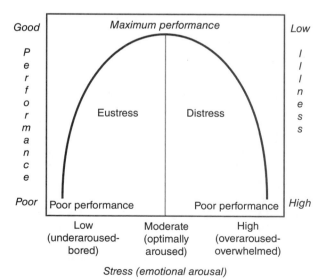

Figure 1.1 The Yerkes-Dodson curve illustrates that, to a point, stress or arousal can actually increase performance. Stress to the left of the midpoint is considered to be eustress. Stress beyond the midpoint, however, is believed to detract from performance and/or health status and is therefore labeled distress.

from eustress to distress, performance or health decreases and there is greater risk of disease and illness. The optimal stress level is the midpoint, prior to where eustress turns into distress. Studies indicate that stress-related hormones in optimal doses actually improve physical performance and mental-processing skills such as concentration, making you more alert. Beyond that optimal level, though, all aspects of performance begin to decrease in efficiency. Physiologically speaking, your health is at serious risk. It would be simple if this optimal level was the same for all people, but it's not. Hence, the focus of any effective stress-management program is twofold: (1) to find out where this optimal level of stress is for you so that it can be used to your advantage rather than becoming a detriment to your health status and (2) to reduce physical arousal levels using both coping skills and relaxation techniques so that you can stay out of the danger zone created by too much stress.

Types of Stressors

Any situation, circumstance, or stimulus that is perceived to be a threat is referred to as a **stressor**, or that which causes or promotes stress. As you might imagine, the list of stressors is not only endless but varies considerably from person to person. Acute stress is often the result of rapid-onset stressors—those that pop up unexpectedly—like a phone call in the middle of the night or the discovery that you have lost your car keys. Usually, the body begins to react before a full analysis of the situation is made, but a return to a state of calm is also imminent. Chronic stressors—those that may give some advance warning yet manage to cause physical arousal anyway—often merit more attention because their prolonged influence on the body appears to be more significant. Much research has been conducted to determine the nature of stressors, and Girdano, Everly, and Dusek have currently divided them into three categories: bioecological, psychointrapersonal, and social.

Bioecological Influences

Chemtrails, global warming, and genetically modified organisms (GMOs) notwithstanding, several biological and ecological factors may trigger the stress response in varying degrees, some of which are outside our awareness. These are external influences, including sunlight, gravitational pull, solar flares, and electromagnetic fields, that affect our biological rhythms. From the field of chronobiology, we learn that these factors affect three categories of biological rhythms: (1) **circadian rhythms**, fluctuations in physiological functions over the course of a 24-hour period (e.g., body temperature); (2) **ultradian rhythms**, fluctuations that occur over less than a 24-hour period (such as stomach contractions and cell divisions); and (3) **infradian rhythms**, changes that occur over periods longer than 24 hours (e.g., the menses). These biological changes are influenced by such natural phenomena as the earth's orbit and axis rotation, which give us periods of light and darkness as well as seasonal differences. A prime example of a **bioecological influence** is **seasonal affective disorder (SAD)**, a condition affecting many people who live at or near the Arctic Circle. Many such people become depressed when they are deprived of sunlight for prolonged periods. Technological changes are also included in this category, an example being jet lag as a result of airplane travel through several time zones. Electrical pollution, environmental toxins, solar radiation, and noise pollution are other potential bioecological influences. GMOs, petrochemicals, synthetic chemicals, and some types of nanotechnology are considered new bioecological threats. In addition, some synthetic food additives may trigger the release of various stress hormones throughout the body. Note that there is a growing opinion among some health practitioners that increased stress levels in the 21st century may be a direct result of our being out of touch with the natural elements that so strongly influence our body's physiological systems. In any case, some of these bioecological factors can be positively influenced by lifestyle changes, including dietary habits, exercise, and the regular practice of relaxation techniques, which bring a sense of balance back into our lives.

Psychointrapersonal Influences

Our current understanding is that **psychointrapersonal influences** make up the greatest percentage of stressors. These are the perceptions of stimuli that we create through our own mental processes. Psychointrapersonal stressors involve those thoughts, values, beliefs, attitudes, opinions, and perceptions that we use to defend our identity or ego. When any of these is challenged, violated, or even changed, the ego is often threatened and the stress response is the outcome. Psychointrapersonal stressors reflect the unique constructs of our personality, and in the words of stress researcher Kenneth Pelletier, they represent "the chasm between the perceived self and the ideal self-image." These influences are the most likely to cause stress. For this reason it becomes imperative to intercept the stress response in the mind before it cascades down as a rush of stress hormones into the body to cause potential damage.

Social Influences

Social influences have long been the subject of research to explain the plight of individuals who are unable to cope with their given environment. Most notable is the issue of overcrowding and urban sprawl. Studies conducted on several species, such as the studies of Roger Allen, have shown that when their numbers exceed the territorial boundary of each animal, despite an abundance of food and water, several seemingly healthy animals die off. This need for personal space appears to be universal in the animal kingdom. This includes humans, who likewise begin to show signs of frustration in crowded urban areas, traffic jams, long lines at checkout stands, or whenever their personal space is "invaded." The origin of this particular social influence may be instinctual in nature. Additional social causes of stress, to name but a few, include financial insecurity, the effects of relocation, some technological advances, violation of human rights, and low socioeconomic status. New to the list of social influences are global warming concerns and water resource issues as the global population increases, taxing our very lifestyles with regard to scarcity issues.

Social Stress in America: A 21st-Century Look

Social influences linked to stress have been studied for decades, most notably by Holmes and Rahe with the **Social Readjustment Rating Scale (SRRS)** and the concept of **life change units (LCUs)**. It was their work that highlighted the list of top life stressors, including death of a spouse, loss of a job, death of a child, divorce, and high mortgage payments. While these stressors haven't changed, the pace of society has quickened to warp speed. With this rapid change, more stressors have been added to the list, and the impact of stress on one's health has been confirmed.

The APA concluded the 2019 Stress in America study by noting that personal sources of stress and American stress levels remain relatively consistent year to year. Furthermore, they noted that those demographically a part of Generation Z (ages 18 to 22), Millennials (ages 23 to 40), or Generation X (ages 41 to 54) cited the most stress, compared to Baby Boomers (ages 53 to 73) and older adults (ages 74 and older).

Although the 2019 study did not specifically enquire about stress management skills, recent Stress in America studies have found that effective coping skills are in short supply. The conclusions drawn from the 2016 and 2017 surveys underscore the relationship between stress and disease/illness and highlight the need for people to harness better stress management skills.

In 2019, neurosurgeon and CNN chief medical correspondent Sanjay Gupta, M.D., filmed a documentary for HBO titled *One Nation Under Stress*. Gupta used the documentary to try to understand why life expectancy in America has fallen so dramatically over the past several years. In 1997, the United States had one of the highest life expectancy rates in the developed world. Times have changed. Mortality rates in the United States are on the increase, and toxic stress has been identified as a unifying factor. With 8 out of 10 people citing stress as a significant part of their daily lives, Gupta concludes that toxic stress is lethal, resulting in what is now called "deaths of despair." Alcoholism and subsequent liver disease, opioid addiction, and suicide top the list for stress-related deaths. Based on his research, Gupta concludes that chronic stress results from (1) feelings of instability and a lack of control over one's life and (2) the fear of downward mobility among the working class. Gupta further states that the American Dream is illusive and that, until social conditions change, stress-related mortality rates will continue to increase.

Similar to the APA's "Stress in America" study, in 2014 National Public Radio and The Kaiser Health Foundation conducted a series titled "The Burden of Stress in America." Here are some of their findings:

- Half of those questioned (over 2,000 people) cited a major stressful experience in the past year.
- Health-related issues are the stressful experiences most frequently mentioned.
- Feelings of being overwhelmed with responsibilities and financial struggles top the list of those who experience the greatest stress.
- Additional stressors included work problems, health problems, family issues, and being unhappy with physical appearances.

This study also looked at common daily stressors and hassles. Topping the list were juggling family schedules, disillusion with government politics, watching/reading/listening to the news, household chores, running errands, car problems, commuting to work, losing smartphones, and using social media.

Whether it be daily hassles or bigger issues, sleep patterns and eating behaviors both were greatly (negatively) impacted by stress. Not all people reported having stress, and among those who appear to cope well, many credit their resilient personality traits, family and friends, spending time outdoors, hobbies, physical exercise, meditation, and time with pets.

Although major life events, such as getting married or relocating for a new job, may be chronic stressors to some, renowned stress researcher **Richard Lazarus** hypothesized in 1984 that the accumulation of acute stressors or **daily life hassles**, such as locking your keys in your car, playing telephone tag, or driving to work every day in traffic, are just as likely to adversely affect one's health as is the death of a spouse. These hassles are often based on unmet expectations that trigger an anger response of some type, whereas stressors of a chronic nature more often than not appear to have a greater association with fear and anxiety. Lazarus defined hassles as "daily interactions with the environment that were essentially negative." He also hypothesized that a balance of emotional experiences—positive emotions as well as negative ones—is necessary, and that people who have no exposure to life's "highs" or emotional uplifts are also susceptible to disease and illness. Further research by Lazarus, Ornstein and Sobel, and others have proved that his hypothesis has significant merit regarding stress and disease. As might be expected, the issue of life-style habits, changes, and hassles as social influences has come under attack by those who argue that perception or cognition plays an important role in the impact of stressors. Suffice it to say that all stressors, regardless of classification, are connected to human well-being in a very profound way.

Although the data regarding the stressful effects of the COVID-19 pandemic have yet to be studied in earnest, no doubt we will see a new chapter on this topic added to the disciplines that examine this powerful social dynamic, one that will certainly change many aspects of work, social interactions, economics, health practices, communication, and much more in the years to come. Already, mental health experts are forecasting a dramatic need for mental health and self-care programs to combat the long-term effects and trauma from the pandemic. Repeated news accounts of death, social isolation, and other factors due to the pandemic have experts warning of a historic mental health crisis with depression, domestic violence, substance abuse, PTSD, and suicide looming over the country's population.

The General Adaptation Syndrome

Following Cannon's lead early in the 20th century, Selye studied the fight-or-flight response, specifically the physiological effects of chronic stress, using rats as subjects. In experiments designed to stress the rats, Selye noted that several physiological adaptations occurred as a result of repeated exposures to stress, adaptations that had pathological repercussions. Examples of these stress-induced changes included the following:

- Enlargement of the adrenal cortex (a gland that produces stress hormones)
- Constant release of stress hormones; corticosteroids released from the adrenal cortex
- Atrophy or shrinkage of lymphatic glands (thymus gland, spleen, and lymph nodes)
- Significant decrease in the white blood cell count
- Bleeding ulcerations of the stomach and colon
- Death of the organism

Many of these changes were very subtle and often went unnoticed until permanent damage had occurred. Selye referred to these collective changes as the **general adaptation syndrome (GAS)**, a process in which the body tries to accommodate stress by adapting to it. From his research, Selye identified three stages of the general adaptation syndrome:

- *Stage 1:* **Alarm reaction**. The alarm reaction describes Cannon's original fight-or-flight response. In this stage several body systems are activated, primarily the nervous system and the endocrine system, followed by the cardiovascular, pulmonary, and musculoskeletal systems. Like a smoke detector alarm buzzing late at night, all senses are put on alert until the danger is over.

- *Stage 2:* **Stage of resistance**. In the resistance stage, the body tries to revert to a state of physiological calm, or homeostasis, by resisting the alarm. Because the perception of a threat still exists, however, complete homeostasis is never reached. Instead, the body stays activated or aroused, usually at a lesser intensity than during the alarm stage but enough to cause a higher metabolic rate in some organ tissues. One or more organs may, in effect, be working overtime and, as a result, enter the third and final stage.

- *Stage 3:* **Stage of exhaustion**. Exhaustion occurs when one (or more) of the organs targeted by specific metabolic processes can no longer meet the demands placed upon it and fails to function properly. This can result in death to the organ and, depending on which organ becomes dysfunctional (e.g., the heart), possibly the death of the organism as a whole.

Selye's general adaptation syndrome outlined the parameters of the physiological dangers of stress. His research opened the doors to understanding the strong relationship between stress and disease and the mind-body-spirit equation. In addition, his work laid the foundation for the utilization of relaxation techniques that have the ability to intercept the stress response, thereby decreasing susceptibility to illness and disease. Congruent with standard medical practice of his day (and even today), initial stress management programs were geared toward reducing or eliminating the symptoms of stress. Unfortunately, this approach has not always proved successful.

Bad Stress in a Good Light

More research has come to light about the stress response, and we now know that the hormone dehydroepiandrosterone (DHEA) is produced and released by the adrenal glands, as is cortisol. **Cortisol** is considered a catabolic (breaks down) hormone, whereas DHEA is considered an anabolic (builds up) hormone. In a perfect world (in which we only experience short-term stress) these two tend to balance each other out. During chronic stress, however, much more cortisol is produced than DHEA. This creates an imbalance that can wreak havoc on the body's physiological systems over time. Kelly McGonigal, author of the popular book *The Upside of Stress*, suggests that if we assume a positive attitude about stress (accept the challenge and rise to the occasion), we can promote a better hormonal balance between cortisol and DHEA. Putting a new spin on the term *fight or flight*, McGonigal refers to the stress response as *excite and delight*, an expression aimed at placing bad stress in a good light, though not all experts agree with her perspective.

Posttraumatic Stress Disorder 101

There is stress and then there is STRESS! Although most people claim to live (or even brag about) stressful lives, the truth of the matter is that few people encounter the truly horrific events of death and carnage. The repeated horrors of war, however, have notoriously ranked at the top of every list as the most unbearable of all stressors that anyone can endure psychologically—and for good reason. To quote Civil War General William T. Sherman, "War is hell." Major stressful events typically include those that threaten one's life, result in serious physical injury, expose one to horrific carnage, or create intense psychological shock, all of which are strongly influenced by the intensity and duration of the devastation either experienced or observed firsthand. The result is an emotional wound embedded in the unconscious mind that is very hard to heal.

Every war seems to have its own name for this type of anxiety disorder. Somber Civil War soldiers were described as having "soldier's heart." Affected military personnel returning from World War I were described as being "shell-shocked." Soldiers and veterans from World War II exhibiting neurotic anxiety were described as having severe "battle fatigue" or "combat fatigue." The term posttraumatic stress disorder—more commonly known as PTSD—emerged during the treatment of soldiers returning from Vietnam who seemed to lack industrial-strength coping skills to deal with the hellacious memories that haunted them both day and night. This emotional disorder was first registered in the *Diagnostic and Statistical Manual of Mental Disorders* (DSM) in 1980 and has been the topic of intense investigation ever since. Sadly, the wars in Iraq and Afghanistan have provided countless case studies for this anxiety disorder.

Although mortal combat ranks at the top of the list of hellacious experiences, one doesn't have to survive a suicide bomber in the streets of Baghdad to suffer from PTSD. Survivors and rescue workers of the World Trade Center and Pentagon catastrophes are known to still be dealing with this trauma, as are several thousand people displaced from the wrath of Hurricanes Katrina and Rita. Violent crime victims, airplane crash survivors, sexual/physical assault victims, and occasionally first responders (e.g., police officers, fire fighters, emergency medical technicians) are also prone to this condition. Given the nature of global warming and climate change and terrorism, it is suggested that PTSD may become a common diagnosis among world citizens, affecting legions of friends, colleagues, and family members alike. Secondary PTSD is a term given to family members, friends, and colleagues who are negatively affected by the ripples of strife experienced by loved ones (even patients) who have had direct exposure to severe trauma.

The symptoms of PTSD include the following: chronic anxiety, nightmares, flashbacks, insomnia, loss of appetite, memory loss, hypervigilance, emotional detachment, clinical depression, helplessness, restlessness, suicidal tendencies, and substance addictions. Typically, a person suffering from PTSD has several of these symptoms at the same time. Whereas the symptoms for some individuals may last for months, for others PTSD becomes a lifelong ordeal, particularly if treatment is avoided, neglected, or shunned. The key to working with PTSD patients is to access the power of the unconscious mind by identifying deep-seated memories so that they may be acknowledged and released in a healthy manner rather than repressed and pushed deeper in the unconscious mind.

Specialists who treat patients with PTSD recommend that treatment begin as soon as possible to prevent a worsening effect. Initial treatment (intervention) is referred to as critical incidence stress management (CISM). The purpose of CISM is to (1) significantly reduce the traumatic effects of the incident and (2) prevent further deep-seated PTSD occurrences. To promote emotional catharsis, specific treatment modalities include eye movement desensitization and reprocessing (EMDR), counseling, and group therapy. The Trauma Recovery Institute cites art therapy, journal writing, and hypnosis as complementary coping skills for emotional catharsis. Many patients are also prescribed medications. Although medications may help reduce anxiety, it should be noted that they do not heal emotional wounds.

Stress and Insomnia

Muscle tension may be the number-one symptom of stress, but in our ever-present, demanding 24/7 society, insomnia runs a close second. Insomnia is best defined as poor-quality sleep, abnormal wakefulness, or the inability to sleep, and it can affect anyone. Overall, Americans get 20 percent less sleep than their 19th-century counterparts. According to a recent survey by the National Sleep Foundation, more than 60 percent of Americans suffer from poor sleep quality, resulting in everything from falling asleep on the job and marital problems to car accidents and lost work productivity. Does your stress level affect your sleep quality? Even if you sleep well, it is hard these days not to notice the proliferation of advertisements for sleep prescriptions, suggesting a serious public health concern.

Numerous studies have concluded that a regular good night's sleep is essential for optimal health, whereas chronic insomnia is often associated with several kinds of psychiatric problems. Emotional stress (the preoccupation with daily stressors) is thought to be a primary cause of insomnia. The result is an anxious state of mind in which thoughts race around, ricocheting from brain cell to brain cell, never allowing a pause in thought processes or allowing the person to nod off.

Many other factors (sleep stealers) detract from one's **sleep hygiene** and can affect the quality of sleep, including hormonal changes (e.g., premenstrual syndrome, menopause), frequent urination, circadian rhythm disturbances (e.g., jet lag), shift work, medication side effects, and a host of lifestyle behaviors (e.g., excessive caffeine intake, little or no exercise, prolonged television watching, alcohol consumption, smartphone use) that infringe on a good night's sleep.

How much sleep is enough to feel recharged? Generally speaking, 8 hours of sleep is the norm, although some people can get as few as 6 hours of sleep and feel fully rested. Others may need as many as 10 hours. New findings suggest that adolescents, including all people up to age 22, need more than 8 hours of sleep.

Not only can stress (mental, emotional, physical, or spiritual) affect the quality and quantity of sleep, but the rebound effect of poor sleep can, in turn, affect stress levels, making the poor sleeper become more irritable, apathetic, or cynical. Left unresolved, the rebound effect can become an unbroken cycle (negative feedback loop). Although many people seek medical help for insomnia and often are given a prescription, drugs should be considered as a last resort. Many (if not all) techniques for stress management, ranging from cardiovascular exercise to meditation, have proven to be effective in promoting a good night's sleep.

The field of sleep research began in earnest more than 60 years ago. Yet, despite numerous studies, the reason we spend approximately one-third of our lives in slumber still baffles scientists. From all appearances, sleep promotes physical restoration. However, when researchers observe sleep-deprived subjects, it's the mind—not the body—that is most affected, with symptoms of poor concentration, poor retention, and poor problem-solving skills.

Insomnia is categorized in three ways: transient (short term with 1 or 2 weeks affected), intermittent (occurs on and off over a prolonged period), and chronic (the inability to achieve a restful night of sleep over many, many months). Although each of these categories is problematic, chronic insomnia is considered the worst.

All-nighters, exam crams, late-night parties, and midnight movies are common in the lives of college undergraduates, but the cost of these behaviors often proves unproductive. Unfortunately, the population of people who seem to need the most sleep, but often get the least amount, are adolescents younger than age 20.

Although sleep may be relaxing, it is important to remember that sleeping is not a relaxation technique. Studies show that heart rate, blood pressure, and muscle tension can rise significantly during the dream state of sleep. What we do know is that effective coping and relaxation techniques greatly enhance one's quality of sleep.

College students are notorious for poor sleep habits. Left unchanged, these habits are carried throughout the life cycle, with some serious health consequences. Here are a few suggestions to improve your sleep quality:

- Avoid drinking any beverages with caffeine after 6:00 p.m., as the effects of caffeine on the nervous system promote a stress response rather than a relaxation effect.
- Physical exertion (cardiovascular exercise) is regarded as a great way to ensure a good night's sleep.
- Keep a regular sleep cycle by going to bed at the same time every night (within 15 minutes) and waking up at about the same time each morning (even weekends).
- Enhance your sleep hygiene. Create a sleep-friendly environment in which bright light and noise are minimized or completely eliminated.
- Avoid watching television right before you go to bed. Instead, try reading—but not with a screen device!
- Make your bedroom a tech-free zone. Avoid using your smartphone or tablet in the bedroom, even as an alarm clock, and turn off your Wi-Fi router before you turn in.

College Stress

What makes the college experience a significant departure from the first 18 years of life is the realization that with the freedom of lifestyle choices come the responsibilities that go with it. Unless you live at home while attending school, the college experience is one in which you transition from a period of dependence (on your parents) to independence. As you move from the known into the unknown, the list of stressors a college student experiences is rather startling. Here is a sample of some of the more common stressors that college students encounter:

- *Roommate dynamics:* Finding a roomate who is compatible is not always easy, especially if you had your own room in your parents' home. As we all know, or will quickly learn, best friends do not make the best roommates, yet roommates can become good friends over time. Through it all, roommate dynamics involve the skills of compromise and diplomacy under the best and worst conditions. Should you find yourself in an untenable situation, campus housing staff will do their best to accommodate you and resolve problems. However, their schedule and yours may not always be the same. For college students who don't leave home, living as an adult in a home in which their parents and siblings are now roommates can become its own form of stress.

- *Professional pursuits:* What major should I choose? Perhaps one of the most common soul-searching questions to be asked in the college years is, What do I want to do for the rest of my life? It is a well-known fact that college students can change majors several times during their college careers, and many do. The problem is compounded when there is parental pressure on you to move toward a specific career path (e.g., law or medicine) or you feel the desire to please your parents by picking a major that they like but you don't.

- *Academic deadlines (exams, papers, and projects):* Academics includes taking midterms and finals, writing research papers, and completing projects. These are, after all, hallmarks of measuring what you have learned. With a typical semester load of 15 to 20 credits, many course deadlines can fall on the same day, and there is the ever-present danger that not meeting expectations can result in poor grades or academic probation.

- *Financial aid and school loans:* If you have ever stood in the financial aid office during the first week of school, you could write a book on the topic of stress. The cost of a college education is skyrocketing, and the pressure to pay off school loans after graduation can make you feel like an indentured servant. Assuming that you qualify for financial aid, you should know that receiving the money in time to pay your bills rarely happens. Problems are compounded when your course schedule gets expunged from computer records because your financial aid check was 2 weeks late. These are just some of the problems associated with financial aid.

- *Budgeting your money:* It's one thing to ask your parents to buy you some new clothes or have them pick up the check at a restaurant. It's quite another when you start paying all your own bills. Learning to budget your money is a skill that takes practice, and learning not to overextend yourself is not only a skill but also an art in these tough economic times. At some time or another, everyone bounces a check. The trick to avoid doing it is not to spend money you do not have and to live within your means.

- *Lifestyle behaviors:* The freedom to stay up until 2:00 a.m. on a weekday, skip a class, eat nothing but junk food, or take an impromptu road trip includes being responsible for these actions. Independence from parental control means balancing freedom with responsibility. Stress enters your life with a vengeance when freedom and responsibility are not balanced.

- *Peer groups and peer pressure (drugs and alcohol):* There is a great need to feel accepted by new acquaintances in college, and this need often leads to succumbing to peer pressure—and in new environments with new acquaintances, peer pressure can be powerful. Stress arises when the actions of the group are incongruent with your own philosophies and values. The desire to conform to the group is often stronger than your willpower to hold your own ground.

- *Exploring sexuality:* Although high school is the time when some people explore their sexuality, this behavior occurs with greater frequency during the college years, when you are away from the confines of parental control and more assertive with your self-expression. With the issue of sexual exploration come questions of values, contraception, pregnancy, homosexuality, bisexuality, AIDS, abortion, acceptance, and impotence, all of which can be very stressful.

- *Friendships:* The friendships made in college have a special quality with bonds that can last a lifetime. As you grow, mature, and redefine your values, your friends, like you, will change, and so will the quality of each friendship. Cultivating a quality relationship takes time, meaning you cannot be good friends with everyone you like. In addition, tensions can quickly mount as the dynamics between you and those in your close circle of friends come under pressure from all the other college stressors.

- *Intimate relationships:* Spending time with one special person with whom you can grow in love is special indeed. But the demands of an intimate relationship are strong, and in the presence of a college environment, intimate relationships are under a lot of pressure. If and when the relationship ends, the aftershock can be traumatic for one or both parties, leaving little desire for one's academic pursuits.

- *Starting a professional career path:* It's a myth that you can start a job making the same salary that your parents make, but many college students believe this to be true. With this myth comes the pressure to equal the lifestyle of one's parents the day after graduation. (This may explain why so many college graduates return home to live after graduation.) The perceived pressures of the real world can become so overwhelming that college seniors procrastinate on drafting a resume or initiating the job search until the week of graduation.

For the nontraditional college student (older than ages 18–22), the problem can be summarized in one word: balance! Trying to balance a job, family, and schoolwork becomes a juggling act extraordinaire. In attempting to satisfy the needs of your supervisor, colleagues, friends, spouse, children, and parents (and perhaps even pets), what usually is squeezed out is time for yourself. In the end everything seems to suffer. Often schoolwork is given a lower priority when addressing survival needs, and typically this leads to feelings of frustration about the inadequacy of time and effort available for assignments or exams. Of course, there are other stressors that cross the boundaries between work, home, and school, all of which tend to throw things off balance as well. Exercises 1.1–1.5 invite you to reflect on these issues.

The Sociology of Stress

Today's world is very different from when Walter Cannon coined the term *fight-or-flight response* and Hans Selye first uttered the words *general adaptation syndrome*. Little did they know just how much stress would become part of the social fabric of everyday life in the 21st century. Some experts argue that our collective stress is a result of our inability to keep up with all the changes that influence the many aspects of our lives. Simply stated, our physiology has not evolved at a comparable rate as the social changes of the last half-century.

Holmes and Rahe, the creators of the Social Readjustment Rating Scale, were dead on about various social aspects that can destabilize one's personal equilibrium, even with the best coping skills employed. Yet no matter what corner of the global village you live in, the stresses of moving to a new city or losing a job are now compounded by significant 21st-century issues. We are a product of our society, and societal stress is dramatically on the rise.

Experts who keep a finger on the pulse of humanity suggest that as rapid as these changes are now, the rate and number of changes are only going to increase.

It's not just the changes we encounter that affect our stress levels, it's how we engage in these new changes. Increasingly, this engagement is online. Unfortunately, the stress that is provoked is real, not virtual. The majority of interactive websites are littered with negative comments, frustrations, expletives, and rants, all of which suggest a malaise in the general public combined with the unparalleled freedom to honestly express oneself anonymously. Being overwhelmed with choices in communication technology for staying in touch with friends, colleagues, and employees leads to a whole new meaning of burnout.

Physiology, psychology, anthropology, theology—the topic of stress is so colossal that it is studied by researchers in a great many disciplines, not the least of which is sociology. Sociology is often described as the study of human social behavior within family, organizations, and institutions: the study of the individual in relationship to society as a whole. Because everybody is born into a family and most people work for a living, no one is exempt from the sociology of stress. Whether we like it or not, we are all connected to each other. Are you a product of your culture? To get a better idea, please complete the survey found in Exercise 1.6.

Perhaps the sociology of stress can best be acknowledged through the newest buzzword—*social networking*—with the likes of Facebook, Twitter, Skype, YouTube, Pinterest, Instagram, as well as new social media and networking outlets taking shape on the cyber-horizon. Technology has even changed how people converse at dinner parties (e.g., one person asks a question and five people pull out their smartphones and Google the answer). Technology, the economy, and the environment have become significant threads of the social fabric.

Technostress

The tsunami of cyber-information has been building for years, yet the first devastating wave seems to have hit the shores of the human mind in earnest about the same time that Facebook hit a billion users in 2010, the same year that the Swiss Army Knife included a USB drive for "survival." Although information overload, privacy, ethics, and bandwidth are issues for many, deeper problems are coming to the surface in the age of iPads and smartphones. The cyber-alchemy of tweets, Facebook updates, Skype messages, text messages, and the deluge of emails has hit a critical mass of annoyance for some and addiction for a great many people who are fed up with giving their lives over to technology. The growing dependence on technology has even inspired a term: *screen addiction*. If it's not computer screens and smartphones, it's iPads and Bluetooth technology, none of which are bad, but they can become problematic if your life is completely centered around being plugged in all the time. The perfect storm of stress is the overwhelming amount of information available, the distractive nature of being plugged in 24/7, a sense of alienation, and the poor boundaries people maintain to regulate this information. The concept of poor boundaries is shown by nearly all college students who text during classroom lectures as well as the scores of people who bring all their technology with them on vacation, thus never separating work from leisure, and possibly compromising both. Similarly, fewer than half of employees nationwide leave their desk/workstation during lunch hour, according to a Manpower survey, leading to higher stress levels and fatigue.

Many terms are used to describe all the problems associated with the tsunami of information and the convenience to access it, but the one term that sums it all up is **technostress**, which is the feeling of being overwhelmed with sensory bombardment from online technology. Factors contributing to technostress include, but are not limited to, privacy issues, identity theft, smartphone radiation, Internet scams, bandwidth, Internet gambling and pornography addiction, and child access to adult content. Perhaps the most widespread stress from technology that most people experience is the perpetual distraction of emails and text messages and the replacement of face-to-face conversation with digital communications.

Research from the University of California at Irvine reveals that the constant interruption of emails triggers the stress response, with the subsequent release of stress hormones affecting short-term memory. If you ever wondered if people, perhaps even yourself, seem addicted to checking emails, voice mails, or tweets, consider this fact: Research shows that the receipt of emails and tweets is accompanied by a release of dopamine. Dopamine, a "feel-good" neurotransmitter, is associated with chemical addictions. In the absence of dopamine release, boredom ensues until the next fix. Every abrupt shift in the history of societies has had its associated stressors—for example, the shift from agrarian to industrial society was correlated with a dramatic increase in alcoholism, regarded as a "social disease" of its time. In today's abrupt shift to online technology and social media, the online technology is itself the addiction.

Young people today who never knew life without a smartphone or iPad don't understand why older adults seem so concerned about their addictive tech habits. Meanwhile, adults now notice that children and teens raised with screen technology may be well versed in cyber-communication skills, yet they are socially immature in face-to-face communication skills, including using eye contact.

Since the advent of smartphones, several new terms have been created to capture the behaviors associated with them. With the phenomenon known as screen addictions, we now have digital toxicity (neurological stress or burnout from the constant engagement [neuroplasticity] with smartphones and other devices). In essence, the brain becomes wired for stress through technology. Digital dementia is a term used to describe people who rely so much on their smartphones and digital devices that they don't give their brains time to store information from short-term to long-term memory. FOMO (fear of missing out) is the term for anxious behaviors associated with an addiction in which the ego needs to be fully engaged with social networking.

Digital Toxicity and Screen Addictions

As more research comes to light about the use of smartphones and screen technology, we are learning how various behaviors with technology affect performance and cognitive skills. What effect does digital overload have on memory? Research reveals that people who had their smartphones within easy reach were less efficient (and apparently more distracted) with a given task than those who did the same task without the presence of their smartphone. Additional studies reveal that students who take notes by hand retain information much better than those who type notes on a computer; they also perform better on exams, suggesting that old-fashioned (analog) note taking is far superior to digital note taking. Smartphones not only distract one's attention—the constant anticipation of social media messages derails memory processing and perhaps other cognitive functions, keeping the brain in an alert state, one in which it is hard to turn off when preparing for sleep. In essence, perpetual use of screen devices trains the brain (via neuroplasticity) to be stressed and anxious. Recommendations from these studies include (1) keeping smartphones off desks, (2) banishing email and text alerts, and (3) scheduling distraction-free periods each day.

The boom in the telecommunications and computer industry—pillars of the information age—have led to an overnight lifestyle change in the United States and global society. In their book Technostress, authors Michelle Weil and Larry Rosen suggest that the rapid pace of technology will only continue with greater speed in the coming years, giving a whole new meaning to the expression 24/7. Their suggestions have proven quite true. They predict, as do others, that the majority of people will not deal well with this change. The result will be more stress, more illness and disease, more addictions, more dysfunction, and a greater imbalance in people's lives. There is general consensus that technology's rate of change has far outpaced the level of responsibility and moral codes that typically accompany the creative process. Exercise 1.6 invites you to examine your technostress level.

The Rise of Incivility

Have you noticed that today people seem quick tempered, impatient, cynical, self-centered, and perhaps even rude at times? If you have, you are not alone. Civility, as expressed through social etiquette, refers to the practice of good manners and appropriate behavior. Many consider basic rules of civility to be sorely lacking in today's culture. Experts attribute the lack of civility to an alchemy of narcissism, political posturing, and a national lack of values, contributing not only to social unease but also to the economic mess that created the Great Recession of 2008. Moreover, a revolution in the way people communicate with each other over the past few years has dramatically changed the social fabric of our culture, particularly how we relate, or fail to relate, to each other in face-to-face situations. Instant accessibility has sown the seeds of impatience. Politeness has given way to rudeness. Internet rants and talk-radio phone calls carry over into face-to-face shouting matches at sporting events, entertainment venues, and political rallies. Social manners (e.g., appropriate behavior and thinking of others first) have become minimal if not obsolete for many people, particularly when bursts of anger perpetuate feelings of victimization. Today's self-centered, narcissistic indulgences have hit an all-time high, many of which are directly related to political incivility. Incivility seems to be a global issue as well. Disturbed by acts of incivility he has seen globally, the Dalai Lama issued a statement in 2017 pleading for what he calls an education of the heart. "Intolerance leads to hatred and division. The new reality is that everyone is interdependent with everyone else. The time has come to understand that we are the same human beings on this planet. Whether we want to or not, we must coexist."

How did things go so wrong? Some people blame poor parenting skills. Many cite talk radio and various news media that broadcast incivility. Others point their finger at the proliferation of technology and the constant self-promotion that seems to go along with it. Many say the perfect storm of "uncivil Americans" is a combination of all these factors. Noting the serious issue of American incivility, Rutgers University has initiated a one-credit course entitled Project Civility, with topics ranging from smartphone etiquette and cyber-bullying to civil sportsmanship and social responsibility. It is likely that other colleges will follow this trend.

According to a study by the *New York Times*, the average young American now spends every waking minute (with the possible exception of school classes) using a smartphone, computer, tablet, television, or other electronic device. Adults appear to be no different. It is not uncommon to see people texting while at movie theaters, talking on smartphones in restaurants (despite signs prohibiting their use), and texting while driving (despite the growing number of state laws banning this behavior). In 2006, researchers at the University of Utah were curious to see if the distraction from smartphone use while driving was similar to driving while under the influence of alcohol. Using driving simulators, it was revealed that people on smartphones show a driving impairment rate similar to a blood alcohol level of 0.08 percent, the demarcation of drunk driving in the majority of states in the United States. Although many people may recognize the dangers of talking and driving, few offer to give up this mode of multitasking.

Many people use technology to avoid stressful situations, again adding to a general lack of civility in society. Examples include quitting a job with a tweet, breaking up with a girlfriend/boyfriend on Facebook, or sending a derogatory email and blind-copying everyone in one's address book. The modern lack of civility cannot be blamed entirely on technology, yet the dramatic rise in the use of communication devices has played its part. How would you rate your current level of social etiquette?

Although any number of Americans may be lacking in the social graces, in the face of global calamities, such as horrific 2018 fires in California or hurricanes along the Atlantic and Gulf coasts, Americans are renowned the world over for giving generously to the needy in faraway lands. However, texting a donation during the Super Bowl for earthquake relief is far different from face-to-face contact and polite social interactions. It's the direct social contact skills that prove to be sorely lacking in American culture today. How good are your social skills in this age of incivility? You can begin to find out by completing Exercises 1.7 and 1.8.

Environmental Disconnect

Even if you don't listen to the news regularly, it's hard to ignore the impact that humanity is having on the state of the planet. With a population exceeding 7 billion, the word *sustainable* has entered the American lexicon with great regularity, even if the concept is largely ignored by most citizens. Modern society can be said to be suffering from an environmental disconnect, a state in which people have distanced themselves so much from the natural environment that they cannot fathom the magnitude of their impact on it. It was predicted many years ago by a great many experts and luminaries that, as humanity distances itself from nature, people will suffer the consequences, primarily in terms of compromised health status. The term *nature deficit disorder* was coined by award-winning author Richard Louv in *Last Child in the Woods* to describe the growing abyss between people and the outdoor world. Kids, as it turns out, would rather play video games or surf online than play outside—where there are no outlets or Wi-Fi access.

"How many angels can dance on the head of a pin?" is an age-old question. Today that imponderable question has become "How many humans can sustainably live on Planet Earth?" It's interesting to note that some of the earliest studies on stress physiology involved placing an abnormally high number of mice in a cage. As their environment, personal space, food availability, and quality of life decreased with each additional occupant, tension increased significantly. The parallels between the environment and behavior of those mice and humans today are unavoidable.

By now pretty much everyone has not only heard of the issues on global warming but also experienced the preliminary effects firsthand: violent storms, warm winters, hotter summers, more intense droughts, and severe weather patterns. The problems related to oil dependence were especially highlighted by the massive 2010 oil spill in the Gulf of Mexico. What has yet to become clear to the average person, however, are the problems with water shortages, an issue that will greatly affect everyone. United Nations Secretary General Ban Ki-moon has repeatedly stated that wars will most likely be fought over water sources during our lifetime. Here are some facts that will impact you now and in the years to come:

- About 97.5 percent of Earth's water is salty, with only 2.5 percent of Earth's water considered fresh.
- Two-thirds of all fresh water is frozen.
- Many Western states (e.g., Texas, Arizona, and California) are draining underground aquifers quicker than they can be restored naturally.
- Many fresh-water streams contain hormones and antibiotics from prescription drugs flushed down toilets and agricultural run-off containing petrochemical fertilizers.
- Americans use approximately 100 gallons of water at home each day, compared to 5 gallons each day in developing nations.
- It takes 2,500 gallons of water to make 1 pound of hamburger and 1,800 gallons to grow enough cotton for a pair of blue jeans.
- Clean water is a huge issue in China, so much so that the country tried (and failed) to license and export fresh water from the Great Lakes region in the United States and Canada.
- The Three Gorges Dam in central China has caused Earth's axis to tilt by nearly an inch.
- Floating plastic islands equal to the size of Texas are being spotted and reported in the Pacific Ocean. Popular beaches and coral reefs in Thailand strewn with plastic are now closed to the public indefinitely.
- Many U.S. cities have dangerous levels of lead in their drinking water. Flint, Michigan, has been without clean water since April 24, 2014.

Perhaps the most subtle warning about this disconnect from our environment is the news that for the first time it has been noted that Americans are not getting enough vitamin D, as explained by nutritionist and New York Times reporter Jane Brody. Vitamin D deficiency is due to a lack of exposure to sunlight and poor dietary habits. Sunlight is often referred to as the sunshine vitamin because, as sunlight reaches the skin, it reacts to help form vitamin D. Today people spend little time outdoors, denying themselves exposure to adequate amounts of sunlight.

Vitamin D isn't the only nutritional/environmental problem. People who saw the documentary film *Food, Inc.* (or who read the book by Karl Weber) are acutely aware that the move away from family farms to industrial farms in the last few decades has greatly compromised the quality of food, primarily chicken and beef, and encouraged the proliferation of products that use high fructose corn syrup. Changes in the food industry, along with inadequate exercise, help explain the recent dramatic increase in obesity levels in the United States. Genetic engineering of food crops is suggested as a primary reason for the decimation of half of the world's bee population, which is creating a problem regarding the pollination of many crops. Bat and frog populations are being decimated as well. The balance of nature is, in no uncertain terms, out of balance.

Some of the world's leading scientists are not optimistic about the future of humanity, given the stresses we have put on our environment and, in turn, ourselves. The fourth *National Climate Assessment*, released at the end of 2018, contained a dire warning for planetary citizens. Severe impacts of global warming and climate change are already being experienced by people all over the world, including the United States, with changes projected to intensify greatly in the years and decades to come. Physicist Stephen Hawking's current outlook for humanity is grim at best, unless we learn to change our ways, and quickly. He stated, "We are entering an increasingly dangerous period in our history. There have been a number of times in the past when survival has been a question of touch and go. We are rapidly depleting the finite natural resources that Earth provides, and our genetic code carries selfish and aggressive instincts." Harvard biologist E. O. Wilson and others now refer to the loss of biodiversity in our modern era as the "sixth mass extinction" on Earth, with hunting and fishing, loss of natural habitat, and pollution as the primary causes, as does Elizabeth Kolbert. Meanwhile, sociologist Jared Diamond, author of the best-selling book *Collapse: How Societies Choose to Fail or Succeed,* has this message: If positive changes are not made with regard to our use of resources and our relationship to our natural environment, we, too, will face extinction.

Not all views of humanity are so dire or fatalistic. Several, in fact, are quite optimistic—with the caveat that we must act now. Consider that of cell biologist and philosopher Bruce Lipton. In his book *Spontaneous Evolution*, he states, "Society is beginning to realize that our current beliefs are detrimental and that our world is in a very precarious position. The new science (the nexus of quantum physics, psychology, and biology) paves a way into a hopeful story of humanity's potential future, one that promotes planetary healing." Lipton uses the model of holism (where all parts are respected and come together for a greater purpose) as the template for his optimism. Lipton is among a growing group of social luminaries, including Barbara Marx Hubbard, Jean Houston, Christine Page, Edgar Mitchell, Elizabeth Sartoris, and Gregg Braden, who share this optimistic paradigm of humanity's shifting consciousness. In the words of rock musician Sting, "Yes, we are in an appalling environmental crisis, but I think as a species, we evolve through crises. That's the only glimmer of hope, really." Exercise 1.1 invites you to evaluate your relationship to the planet's health.

Race and Gender Stress

One cannot address the sociology of stress without acknowledging race and gender stress. The United States, a nation in large part of immigrants, has often been described as a melting pot, but recently another metaphor has been used to describe the makeup of its citizens: a tossed salad, in which assimilation meets cultural diversity head on. Race and ethnic issues continually make headline news with regard to illegal immigration issues nationwide, disenfranchised black voters in Florida, poverty in New Orleans, horrific acts of anti-Semitism, and Muslim Americans facing episodes of discrimination, to name a few. To this we can add the daily impact and fallout of the #MeToo movement. Race and gender tensions, however, are not new—it could be argued that they are as old as humanity itself.

Since the beginning of time, people have been threatened by people with different skin color, ethnicity, gender, or sexual preference. The 2008 election of the first African American president helped to jumpstart a national discussion on race, but it hasn't resolved the issue of intolerance. Like race issues, gender issues (and to this we can add sexual orientation issues) are also threads in the social fabric once dominated by a white patriarchal society, yet this is changing. Despite the demographic shifts, the dated cultural perceptions of superiority/inferiority persist, and with them the biases that go with them.

Stress, you will remember, is defined as a perceived threat, a threat generated by the ego. These threats manifest in a variety of ways including stereotyping, prejudice, discrimination, harassment, and even physical harm. Race and gender stress may begin early in life, too; many children can attest to being bullied in school or excluded and teased by social cliques. The emotional stress associated with this type of angst can result in low self-esteem, alienation, and anxiety—everybody wants to be accepted.

How can society help alleviate race and gender stress? Anti-bullying programs are being implemented in many schools nationwide, helping raise awareness among kids and parents to the dangers of bullying. On television, many shows have tried to better reflect the demographics of American society with casts of various ethnicities. These are steps in the right direction, and although school curricula and television shows alone cannot change the world overnight, they're a start. Remember that when people demonstrate a bias toward race, gender, ethnic background, or anything related to them, they are projecting their fears. A common reaction is to meet stress with stress, but the best answer is to rise above it and take the high road of integrity.

Stress in a Changing World

Before the coronavirus pandemic of 2020, it was easy to see that people lived very stressed lives as they gazed incessantly at their screen devices at all hours of the day. Gallup Poll surveys, NPR reports, and APA studies all have pointed to the perfect storm of stress with severe health implications. As with the Puritan ethic (worth equals worth) being so strong in the United States, the lion's share of stress was associated with one's job, career, and means to make a living, as many people suffered massive student loan debt and lived in the basements of their family home. Stress grabbed the national headlines repeatedly, so much so that it became nicknamed the "black death" of the 21st century by many people both in the United States and abroad. Cries for work–life balance could be heard coming from all corners of corporate America. Millennials and Gen Z have not fared well with job stress. In a 2019 survey published by Mindsharepartners.org, half of Millennials and 75 percent of Gen Zers left a job partially for mental health reasons. And while people in these demographics are more comfortable about admitting mental health issues, they are also more susceptible to social media stress leading to issues of isolation, alienation; the precursors for depression.

The 2019 APA annual report "Stress in America" found that 91 percent of Generation Z noted physical and/or emotional symptoms of stress, including depression, anxiety, and frustration. Gun violence, constant political bickering and partisanship, economic uncertainty, ecological dystopia, and social media influences all played a role in this new stress equation as well. It was learned through the "Stress in America" that Gen Zers have high levels of loneliness, often substitute social media relationships for actual friendships and support groups, are under constant bombardment by negative self-comparisons, and have an attitude that underlies "destructive perfectionism and all-or-none thinking, all of which leads to poor mental health and embeds a cloud of chronic stress over their heads."

With the lockdowns and self-quarantine imposed by the COVID-19 pandemic, where people had time to examine lifestyle choices, many people (as observed with repeated memes on social media) began to question if they really wanted to return to a fast-paced, tech-heavy lifestyle. Some people enjoyed working from home and not spending 1 to 2 hours a day in traffic. As mentioned, the changes ahead for Americans (and the rest of the world) as we adapt to the "new normal" in a post-pandemic world are yet to be seen. It is fairly certain that with more change will come more frustration, anxiety, and stress as everyone learns to adapt to new and increased stress in an uncertain and rapidly changing world. Yet where there is despair, there is also compassion. Destruction and personal loss from countless natural disasters and the horrors of domestic terrorism have also brought out the best in some people, as scores of individuals and service organizations have come to the aid of their fellow human beings in both their own communities and across the globe. The darkest times can bring out our finest hour, if we transition from fear to compassion.

The Power of Adaptation

One of the greatest attributes of the human species is the ability to adapt to change. Adaptation is the number-one skill we have or coping with the stress of life. Adaptation involves a great many human attributes, from resiliency and creativity to forgiveness, patience, and many, many more. Given the rapid rate of change in the world today, combined with the typical changes one goes through in a lifetime, the ability to adapt is essential. Those who incorporate a strategy to adapt positively will be healthier and also, in the long run, much happier. Adaptation to stress means making small changes in your personal lifestyle so that you can flow with the winds of change taking place in the world and not feel personally violated or victimized. Sometimes adaptation to change means merely fine-tuning a perception or attitude. In the best stress management program reduced to 27 words, the following quote attributed to Reinhold Niebuhr speaks to this process: "God, grant me the serenity to accept the things I cannot change, the courage to change the things I can, and the wisdom to know the difference." The skills introduced in this text are designed to help you gracefully adapt to the winds of change.

The Premise of Holistic Stress Management

Honoring the premise of this ageless wisdom, holistic stress management promotes the integration, balance, and harmony of one's mind, body, spirit, and emotions for optimal health and well-being. Stress affects all aspects of the wellness paradigm. To appreciate the dynamics of the whole, sometimes it's best to understand the pieces that make up the whole. What follows is a definition of each of the four aspects that constitute the human entity and the effect that unresolved stress plays on each:

- *Emotional well-being:* The ability to feel and express the entire range of human emotions, and to control them, not be controlled by them. Unresolved stress tends to perpetuate a preponderance of negative emotions (anger and fear), thus compromising emotional balance and causing the inability to experience and enjoy moments of joy, happiness, and bliss.
- *Physical well-being:* The optimal functioning of the body's physiological systems (e.g., cardiovascular, endocrine, reproductive, immune). Not only does unresolved stress create wear and tear on the body, but the association between stress and disease is approximately 80–85 percent. Ultimately, stress can kill.
- *Mental well-being:* The ability of the mind to gather, process, recall, and communicate information. Stress certainly compromises the ability to gather, process, recall, and communicate information.
- *Spiritual well-being:* The maturation of higher consciousness as represented through the dynamic integration of three facets: relationships, values, and a meaningful purpose in life. Most, if not all, stressors involve some aspect of relationships, values (or value conflicts), and the absence of, search for, or fulfillment of a meaningful purpose in one's life.

The circle is a universal symbol of wholeness, often divided into four parts: north/south/east/west or spring/summer/winter/fall. Mind, body, spirit, and emotions are also four quadrants that make up the whole, often depicted in a circle. Exercise 1.10 invites you to reflect on the concept of wholeness via this symbol so prevalent in world culture.

The Nature of Holistic Stress Management

With the appreciation that the whole is always greater than the sum of its parts, following are some insights that collectively shine light on the timeless wisdom of the nature of holistic stress management:

- Holistic stress management conveys the essence of uniting the powers of the conscious and unconscious minds to work in unison (rather than in opposition) for one's highest potential. In addition, a holistic approach to coping effectively with stress unites the functions of both the right and left hemispheres of the brain.
- Holistic stress management suggests a dynamic approach to one's personal energy in which one lives consciously in the present moment, rather than feeling guilty about things done in the past or worrying about things that may occur in the future.
- Holistic stress management underlies the premise of using a combination of **effective coping skills** to resolve issues that can cause perceptions of stress to linger and **Effective relaxation techniques** to reduce or eliminate the symptoms of stress and return the body to homeostasis. This is different from the standard practice of merely focusing on symptomatic relief.

- Holistic stress management achieves a balance between the role of the ego to protect and the purpose of the soul to observe and learn life's lessons. More often than not, the ego perpetuates personal stress through control and manipulation.
- Holistic stress management is often described as moving from a motivation of fear to a place of unconditional love.

When all of these aspects of holistic stress management are taken into consideration, the process of integrating, balancing, and bringing harmony to mind, body, spirit, and emotions becomes much easier, and arriving at the place of inner peace is easier to achieve.

Chapter Summary

- The advancement of technology, which promised more leisure time, has actually increased the pace of life so that many people feel stressed to keep up with this pace.
- Lifestyles based on new technological conveniences are now thought to be associated with several diseases, including coronary heart disease (CHD) and cancer.
- *Stress* is a term from the field of physics, meaning "physical force" or "tension placed on an object." It was adopted after World War II to signify psychological tension.
- Eastern and Western philosophies, as well as several academic disciplines, including psychology and physiology, offer many definitions of stress. The separation of mind-body is giving way today to a holistic philosophy involving the mental, physical, emotional, and spiritual components of well-being.
- Cannon coined the term *fight-or-flight response* to describe the immediate effects of physical stress. This response is now considered by many to be inappropriate for nonphysical stressors.
- There are three types of stress: eustress (good), neustress (neutral), and distress (bad). There are two types of distress: acute (short-term) and chronic (long-term); the latter is thought to be more detrimental because the body does not return to a state of complete homeostasis.
- Stressors have been categorized into three groups: (1) bioecological influences, (2) psychointrapersonal influences, and (3) social influences.
- Holmes and Rahe created the Social Readjustment Rating Scale (SSRS) to identify major life stressors. They found that the incidence of stressors correlated with health status.
- Selye coined the term *general adaptation syndrome* to explain the body's ability to adapt negatively to chronic stress.
- Females are wired for fight-or-flight, and they also have a tend-and-befriend survival dynamic, a specific nurturing aspect that promotes social support in stressful times.
- The association between stress and insomnia is undeniable. The United States is said to be a sleep-deprived society, but techniques for stress management, including physical exercise, biofeedback, yoga, and diaphragmatic breathing, are proven effective to help promote a good night's sleep.

- Stress can appear at any time in our lives, but the college years offer their own types of stressors because it is at this time that one assumes more (if not complete) responsibility for one's lifestyle behaviors. Stress continues through retirement with a whole new set of stressors in the senior years.
- Sociology is described as the study of human social behavior within family, organizations, and institutions. Societal stress is a force to be reckoned with in today's culture. No one is exempt from the sociology of stress.
- *Techno-stress* is a term used to describe the overwhelming frustrations of sensory bombardment and poor boundaries with the plethora of technological gadgets. Technostress began with personal computers but has evolved with the advent of and addiction to social networking. The body's physiology wasn't designed to be "on" all the time. The result can be burnout and physical health issues.
- Social stress includes a decline in social etiquette. A lack of civility, demonstrated by rude, impatient behavior, is on a dramatic rise in the United States.
- Experts suggest that one aspect of societal stress is an environmental disconnect: a growing disregard of the environment by humanity, such that dramatic changes, from dwindling supplies of fresh water to declining food quality to environmental pollution, will all have a significant impact on each individual's lifestyle and health.
- Racial inequality, racial and gender issues have always been part of the social fabric in the United States and continue to contribute largely to stress, especially as people express themselves with reckless abandon in the digital age.
- Previous approaches to stress management have been based on the **mechanistic model**, which divided the mind and body into two separate entities. The paradigm on which this model was based is now shifting toward a holistic paradigm, in which the whole is greater than the sum of the parts, and the whole person must be treated by working on the causes as well as the symptoms of stress.
- Effective stress-management programs must address issues related to mental (intellectual), physical, emotional, and spiritual well-being.

Additional Resources

Allen, R. *Human Stress: Its Nature and Control.* Edina, MN: Burgess Intl Group; 1983.

Allen, M., Ken Burns: Coronavirus pandemic is a crisis "on the level" of the Civil War and Great Depression. Axio.com May 25, 2020. https://www.axios.com/ken-burns-coronavirus-transition-lab-podcast-4e247105-896e-4a2e-953f-7d4f6b9943c3.html

Allen, M. Ken Burns: Coronavirus Pandemic Is a Crisis "On the Level" of the Civil War and Great Depression. Axios.com. May 25, 2020. https://www.axios.com/ken-burns-coronavirus-transition-lab-podcast-4e247105-896e-4a2e-953f-7d4f6b9943c3.html. Accessed November 23, 2020.

American Heart Association. www.heart.org.

American Institute of Stress. America's #1 Health Problem. January 4, 2017. https://www.stress.org/americas-1-health-problem. Accessed November 23, 2020.

American Psychological Association. *Stress in America: Paying with Our Health.* February 4, 2015. http://www.apa.org/news/press/releases/stress/2014/stress-report.pdf. Accessed November 12, 2020.

American Sleep Apnea Association (Sleephealth.org). Insufficient Sleep Is a Public Health Epidemic – CDC. https://www.sleephealth.org/sleep-health/the-state-of-sleephealth-in-america. Accessed November 23, 2020.

Beckford, M. Working Nine to Five Is Becoming a Thing of the Past. *The Daily Telegraph*. May 4, 2007.

Bernstein, A. *The Myth of Stress*. New York: Simon & Schuster; 2010.

Brody, J. E. What Do You Lack? Probably Vitamin D. *New York Times*. July 26, 2010. www.nytimes .com/2010/07/27/health/27brod.html. Accessed November 12, 2020.

Brown, L. *Plan B: Rescuing a Planet Under Stress and a Civilization in Trouble*. New York: Norton; 2006.

Carlson, R. *Don't Sweat the Small Stuff*. New York: Hyperion Books; 1997.

Carr, N. *The Shallows: What the Internet Is Doing to Our Brains*. New York: W. W. Norton; 2011.

Centers for Disease Control and Prevention (CDC). Heart Disease Facts. https://www.cdc.gov/heart-disease/facts.htm. Accessed November 23, 2020.

Chatterjee, R., & Wroth, C. WHO Redefines Burnout as a 'Syndrome' Linked with Chronic Stress. May 28, 2019. https://www.npr.org/sections/health-shots/2019/05/28/727637944/who-redefines -burnout-as-a-syndrome-linked-to-chronic-stress-at-work. Accessed November 23, 2020.

Cloud, J. The Top 10 Everything of 2008. 6. Staycation. November 3, 2008. http://content.time.com/ time/specials/packages/article/0,28804,1855948_1864100_1864106,00.html. Accessed November 23, 2020.

Dawson, P. *Sleep and Adolescents*. January 2005. http://www.nasponline.org/resources/principals /sleep%20disorders%20web.pdf. Accessed November 12, 2020.

Diamond, J. *Collapse: How Societies Choose to Fail or Succeed*. New York: Penguin Books; 2011.

Dossey, L. Plugged In: At What Price? The Perils and Promise of Electrical Communications. *Explore* 5(5): 257–262, 2009.

Eisenberg, D., et al. Trends in Alternative Medicine Use in the United States, 1990–1997: Results of a Follow-up National Survey. *JAMA 280*: 1569–1575, 1998.

Eisenberg, D., et al. Unconventional Medicine in the United States. *New England Journal of Medicine 328*: 246–252, 1993.

Expedia.com *2009 International Vacation Deprivation™ Survey Results*. March 19, 2009. https:// media.expedia.com/media/content/expus/graphics/promos/vacations/Expedia_International _Vacation_Deprivation_Survey_2009.pdf. Accessed November 12, 2020.

Fielding, J. Americans Aren't Getting Enough Sleep and It's Killing Us. The Hill. March 30, 2019. https://thehill.com/opinion/healthcare/436555-americans-arent-getting-enough-sleep-and-its-killing-us. Accessed November 23, 2020.

Gallwey, W. I. *The Inner Game of Stress*. New York: Random House; 2009.

Gil Institute for Trauma Recovery and Education. Fairfax, Virginia. http://www.gilinstitute.com. Accessed November 23, 2020.

Girdano, D., Everly, G., & Dusek, D. *Controlling Stress and Tension*. Upper Saddle River, NJ: Benjamin Cummings; 2012.

Gyatso, T. *Op-Ed: Dalai Lama: We Need an Education of the Heart*. *Los Angeles Times*. November 13, 2017. https://www.latimes.com/opinion/op-ed/la-oe-dalai-lama-alt-we-need-an-education-of-the -heart-20171113-story.html. Accessed November 12, 2020.

Heid, M. How Is Covid-19 Affecting Our Mental Health. TIME. May 25, 2020.

Hibbs, J., & Rostain, A. Why 90 Percent of Generation Z Says They're Stressed Out. Psychology Today. December 27, 2018. https://www.psychologytoday.com/us/blog/the-stressed-years-their-lives/201812/why-90-percent-generation-z-says-theyre-stressed-out. Accessed November 23, 2020.

HRM Guide. *Overworked Americans Can't Use Up Their Vacation*. May 13, 2002. http://www .hrmguide.net/usa/worklife/unused_vacation.htm. Accessed November 12, 2020.

Hull, M. Stress Facts and Statistics. The Recovery Village. April 7, 2020. Updated November 6 2020. https://www.therecoveryvillage.com/mental-health/stress/related/stress-statistics. Accessed November 23, 2020.

Jonas, W., Developing an Integrative Health Model: Who, What, and How. September 2017. https:// drwaynejonas.com/wp-content/uploads/2017/09/IntegrativeHealthReferralGuide_09.20.17_ web.pdf. Accessed November 23, 2020.

Kolbert, E., The Sixth Extinction. Picador Publishers, New York. 2015.

Krugman, M. *The Insomnia Solution*. New York: Grand Central Publishing; 2009.

Lallas, N. *Renewing Values in America*. Mill Valley, CA: Artis Press; 2009.

Lazarus, R. Puzzles in the Study of Daily Hassles. *Journal of Behavioral Medicine* 7: 375–389, 1984.

Levy, S. Facebook Grows Up. *Newsweek*. August 20, 2007: 41–46.

Lipton, B. *Keynote Address: Get Your Shift Together*. Loveland, CO. July 18, 2012.

Lipton, B., & Bhaerman, S. *Spontaneous Evolution*. Carlsbad, CA: Hay House; 2010.

Louv, R. *Last Child in the Woods*. Chapel Hill, NC: Algonquin; 2008.

Luskin, F., & Pelletier, K. *Stress Free for Good: 10 Scientifically Proven Life Skills for Health and Happiness*. New York: HarperOne; 2009.

Maas, J. *Sleep for Success*. Indianapolis, IN: AuthorHouse; 2011.

Maas, J., & Davis, H. *Sleep to Win!* Indianapolis, IN: AuthorHouse; 2013.

Marquardt, K. Take a True Lunch Break. *U.S. News and World Report*. December 2010.

McEwen, B. *The End of Stress as We Know It*. Washington, DC: Joseph Henry Press; 2002.

McGonigal, K. *The Upside of Stress: Why Stress Is Good for You and How You Can Get Good at It*. New York: Avery Books; 2015.

McMaster, G. Millennials and Gen Z Are More Anxious Than Previous Generations: Here's Why. Folio. January 28, 2020. https://www.folio.ca/millennials-and-gen-z-are-more-anxious-than-previous-generations-heres-why. Accessed November 23, 2020.

Mehar, P. Negative Mood Signals Body's Immune Response. Tech Explorist. December 21, 2018. https://www.techexplorist.com/negative-mood-signals-bodys-immune-response/19606. Accessed November 23, 2020.

Meyer, D. *Why We Hate Us: American Discontent in the New Millennium*. New York, NY: Crown; 2009.

Mind Share Partners. https://www.mindsharepartners.org/

Mitchum Report on Stress in the 90's. New York: Research and Forecast Inc.; 1990.

Moyers, B. *Healing and the Mind*. Public Broadcasting System; 1993.

Moyers, B. *Healing and the Mind*. New York: Doubleday; 1995.

National Geographic (Special Issue). Water: Our Thirsty World. April 2010.

National Public Radio. Stressed-Out (Special Series). 2014. http://www.npr.org/series/327816692/stressed-out. Accessed November 12, 2020.

National Sleep Foundation. Lack of Sleep Is Affecting Americans Finds the National Sleep Foundation. December 2014. https://www.sleepfoundation.org/press-release/lack-sleep-affecting-americans-finds-national-sleep-foundation. Accessed November 23, 2020.

National Sleep Foundation. Sleep in America Poll 2020: Americans Feel Sleepy 3 Days a Week with Impacts on Activities, Mood and Acuity. Sleepfoundation.org. 2020. https://www.sleepfoundation.org/wp-content/uploads/2020/03/SIA-2020-Q1-Report.pdf?x41620. Retrieved November 23, 2020.

NPR, Robert Wood Johnson Foundation, & Harvard School of Public Health. *The Burden of Stress in America*. 2014. https://media.npr.org/documents/2014/july/npr_rwjf_harvard_stress_poll.pdf. Accessed November 12, 2020.

Ornstein, R., & Sobel, D. *Healthy Pleasures*. Reading, MA: Addison Wesley; 1990.

Perman, C. *Argggh! American Workers Are at a Breaking Point*. April 9, 2013. Business on NBCnews.com. www.cnbc.com/id/100624671. Accessed January 7, 2021.

Quintos, N. Vacation-deficit disorder. *National Geographic Traveler*. November/December 2007: 22–27.

Ray, J. Americans' Stress, Worry and Anger Intensified in 2018. Gallup News Poll. April 25, 2019. https://news.gallup.com/poll/249098/americans-stress-worry-anger-intensified-2018.aspx. Accessed November 23, 2020.

Rohleder, N. Chronic Stress and Disease (Chapter 9). In I. Berczi (Ed.), *Insights to Neuroimmune Biology* (pp. 201–214, 2nd ed.), 2016. https://www.sciencedirect.com/science/article/pii/B9780128017708000094. Accessed November 23, 2000.

Rubinkam, M. *During Boring Classes, Texting Is the New Doodling*. Associated Press. November 26, 2010. http://archive.boston.com/news/nation/articles/2010/11/26/during_boring_classes_texting_is_the_new_doodling. Accessed November 12, 2020.

Sapolsky, R. M. *Why Zebras Don't Get Ulcers*. New York: W. H. Freeman; 2004.

Schlitz, M. Personal Communication. December 10, 2018.

Seaward, B. L. *A Good Night's Sleep*. Omaha, NE: WELCOA Books; 2016.

Seigler, K. *Tweeting with the Birds: Pitch Tent, Switch to Wi-Fi*. August 3, 2010. www.npr.org/templates/story/story.php?storyId=128697566. Accessed November 12, 2020. May 15, 2019.

Selye, H. *The Stress of Life*. New York: McGraw-Hill; 1978.

Simeons, A. W. *Man's Presumptuous Brain: An Evolutionary Interpretation of Psychosomatic Disease*. New York: Dutton; 1961.

Simon, S. *Using Your BlackBerry Off-Hours Could Be Overtime*. NPR. August 14, 2010. www.npr.org /templates/story/story.php?storyId=129184907. Accessed November 12, 2020.

Slavish, D., Graham-Engeland, J., Smyth, J. M., & Engeland, C. Salivary Markers of Inflammation in Response to Acute Stress. *Brain Behavior and Immunity 44*: 253–269, February 2015. https://www.sciencedirect.com/science/article/abs/pii/S0889159114004255. Accessed November 23, 2020.

Smith, R., & Lourie, B. *Slow Death by Rubber Duck: The Secret Danger of Everyday Things*. Berkeley, CA: Counterpoint; 2011.

Solly, M. Nearly One-Third of Americans Sleep Fewer Than Six Hours Per Night. *Smithsonian Magazine*. December 26, 2018. https://www.smithsonianmag.com/smart-news/almost-one-third-americans-sleep-fewer-six-hours-night-180971116. Accessed November 23, 2020.

Stepp, L. S. Enough Talk, Already: At Some Point, Experts Say, Taking Action Is Better. *The Journal Times*. September 4, 2007. https://journaltimes.com/lifestyles/enough-talk-already-at-some -point-experts-say-taking-action/article_89fbf8e2-8979-5524-899c-41e7e4f4e86c.html. Accessed November 12, 2020.

Stuart, H. *Stephen Hawking to Human Race: Move to Outer Space or Face Extinction (VIDEO)*. August 6, 2010. https://www.huffpost.com/entry/stephen-hawking-to-human_n_673387. Accessed November 12, 2020.

Swartz, J. Survey Warns of E-mail Stress. *USA Today*. July 16, 2010. http://content.usatoday.com/ communities/technologylive/post/2010/07/e-mail-stress-when-is-too-much-e-mail-too-much /1#.XOaePS2ZPOS. Accessed November 12, 2020.

Taylor, S. *The Tending Instinct*. New York: Owl Books; 2003.

The American Institute of Stress. www.stress.org.

U.S. Global Change Research Program. *Fourth National Climate Assessment: Volume II: Impacts, Risks, and Adaptation in the United States*. Washington, DC. 2018. https://nca2018.globalchange. gov/?fbclid=IwAR3Pinm5_RB76Oi7WmJTLyfn2Kvggva9OVdx8anBgIKjoTDw4kiq3_M9q9I. Accessed November 12, 2020.

Wan W. The Coronavirus Pandemic Is Pushing America into a Mental Health Crisis. *Washington Post*. May 4, 2020. https://www.washingtonpost.com/health/2020/05/04/mental-health-corona virus. Accessed November 23, 2020.

Weil, M., & Rosen, L. *Technostress: Coping with Technology @ Work @ Home @ Play*. New York: John Wiley & Sons; 1998.

Wong, M. Vacationing Americans Have Given New Meaning to the Advertising Slogan, Don't Leave Home Without It. Associated Press. September 1, 2000.

World Health Organization (WHO). *World Health Report*. July 31, 2008. https://www.who.int /whr/2008/en. Accessed November 21, 2020.

World Health Organization. Burn-out an "Occupational Phenomenon": International Classification of Diseases. May 28, 2019. https://www.who.int/mental_health/evidence/burn-out/en. Accessed November 23, 2020.

World Health Organization. As quoted in Spirituality, Happiness and Health. *Christian News Notes*. New York, 1991.

CHAPTER 2

The Psychology of Stress

KEY TERMS

Calculated risk taker
Codependent personality
Cognitive distortion
Defense mechanisms
Ego
Energy psychology

Freud
Hardy personality
Mental well-being
Survivor personality
Type A personality

For eons, philosophers, scientists, theologians, psychologists, and countless other planetary citizens have all wondered, hypothesized, and speculated on the topic of the human mind. What is it? Where is it? How does it work? Why do identical twins have different minds and personalities? Where does the mind go when we die? What is a premonition? Can the mind be trained? What is intelligence? What is conscience? How fast can the mind travel? What is a thought?

In the early decades of the 21st century, scientists have begun to confirm what the mystics stated long ago: The mind is a reservoir of conscious energy that surrounds and permeates the human body. From a holistic perspective, the mind and the brain are not the same thing. The mind, the quintessential seat of consciousness, merely uses the brain as its primary organ of choice. With new revelations from organ transplant recipients (some of whom exhibit changes in personality), apparently the mind uses other organs as well. In fact, new research suggests that every cell has consciousness, giving rise to a new term, *cell memory*.

The study of the mind (and the brain) has led to a deeper understanding of human consciousness, yet it's fair to say that through this vast exploration of dreams, cognitive inventories, hypnosis, meditation, DNA, EEGs, and MRIs, our knowledge, at best, is still embryonic. Current research in the field of consciousness reveals interesting insights about a phenomenon that only grows more fascinating with further study. For example, distant healing, remote viewing, premonitions, synchronicities, near-death experiences, out-of-body experiences, spontaneous healings, and much more only begin to substantiate that mind, as consciousness, is certainly not a simple consequence of brain chemistry, though there are many who still believe it is.

In recent years, a great deal of research has focused on the brain in an effort to understand the workings of the mind. Through hundreds of studies using functional magnetic resonance imaging (fMRI), neuroscientists have made some remarkable discoveries about various thought processes and where they take place in the brain, from the amygdala to the executive function of the prefrontal cortex.

This much we do know: Much like a laptop computer, mental well-being is the ability to gather, process, recall, and communicate information. We also know that stress compromises the mind's ability to do all of these functions. Information is constantly gathered and processed through the portals of the five senses for a variety of reasons (from threats to simple curiosity). Yet it's no secret that information comes into the conscious mind in other ways, including intuition, meditation, and what can only be explained as "extrasensory perception." Just as we know that the mind can generate stress without any outside stimulus, the power of the mind to heal the body is also well documented. Although no one book can begin to elaborate on the psychology of stress or the secrets to **mental well-being**, the following offers some keen insights into the psychology of stress, as observed by renowned leaders in the field who have shared the greatest wisdom to date on the mysteries of the mind.

The Anatomy of Ego

When it comes to the mind, one cannot look at stress without first examining the role of the mind's censor, the **ego**. Many claim that the ego is the cause of both personal and worldly problems, and although this may not be far from the truth, it must also be recognized that the ego is not always bad either. A healthy ego generates high self-esteem. As **Freud** accurately pointed out, the ego serves a role of protection. It also constitutes one's identity (or, as Freud stated, id-entity). Perhaps more accurately, the ego is the mind's bodyguard and censor. In an effort to protect one from harm, the ego sounds the alarm of imminent danger for mental, emotional, and physical threats. Stated simply, it is the ego that trips the fight-or-flight response when one feels threatened. Sometimes the ego goes overboard in its role as the mind's bodyguard and tends to make mountains out of molehills. Experts in the field of psychology call this **cognitive distortion**.

The ego has many "tricks" for protection. Freud called these **defense mechanisms**—thoughts and behaviors that act to decrease pain and perhaps even increase pleasure in the mind and body. He said that, by and large, we use more than one defense mechanism at a time, and for the most part we are not even aware of it. Here is a quick overview of some of the more common defenses of the ego:

- *Denial:* I didn't do it!
- *Repression:* I don't remember doing it!
- *Projection:* He did it!
- *Displacement:* He made me do it!
- *Rationalization:* Everyone does it!
- *Humor:* I did it, and a year from now maybe I'll laugh about this!

At its best, the ego serves as the bodyguard for the soul. At its worst, the ego tries to manipulate everything (and perhaps everybody) through control dramas. When ruled by fear and anger, the ego transitions from a place of power to control, or what some people refer to as the unhealthy ego. Freud might have been the first person in the West to study this aspect of the mind, but he certainly wasn't the first to acknowledge it. Philosophers as far back as ancient Greece, India, China, and Tibet often spoke of the mind's shadow side. In Eastern culture, the ego is called the small mind (also called the false self), and ancient traditions suggest that the best means for mental well-being is to domesticate the small mind so that it can work in harmony with the larger mind of the universe. Psychologist Carl Jung described this process as "embracing the shadow." Ultimately, this means moving beyond a motivation of fear toward a motivation of love and compassion, a process that is not impossible but requires much discipline.

In terms of coping with the perceptions of stress rather than using a defense mechanism to avoid it, the holistic approach to stress management suggests following advice from the Eastern tradition by learning to domesticate the ego. Meditation is the premier skill to accomplish this goal. Exercise 2.1 can also help you start with this process.

The Power of Two Minds

Metaphorically speaking, you have not one but two minds: the conscious mind and the unconscious mind. The conscious mind is best described as an awareness, like that which appears on your computer screen, and it receives nearly all of the attention of the ego. The unconscious mind is analogous not only to that which appears on your hard drive but, some would say, the entire Internet as well. Like an iceberg with nearly 90 percent of its entirety below water, the total mind is vast. It contains a wealth of information that often is never realized, yet it is the model for today's typical computer. Unlike the conscious mind, which shuts down when you sleep, the unconscious mind works 24 hours a day, every day of your life. It, too, offers a sense of awareness. It is a reservoir of endless wisdom as well as a container of all your personal memories (see **Figure 2.1**).

It would be a simple matter if these two minds spoke the same language, but unfortunately this is not the case. Whereas the conscious mind is fluent in verbal skills, linear thinking, rational thinking, and many, many other cognitive functions that are now associated with the left hemisphere of the brain, the unconscious mind is fluent in cognitive skills associated with the right brain: intuition, imagination, and acceptance. Like a virus scanner on your computer, the ego serves the role of censor and gatekeeper, making sure nothing bubbles up to the surface of the conscious mind that might prove to be a threat. Unfortunately, much of this wisdom never passes through the gates of the ego. In no uncertain terms, stress can be defined as the conflict between the conscious and unconscious minds.

It was Carl Jung, one-time protégé of Sigmund Freud, who began, in earnest, to study the workings of the unconscious mind, particularly through dream analysis but also through artwork and other nonverbal means of communication. Jung was of the opinion that if people took the time to learn the language of the unconscious mind, often expressed in archetypal symbols and, in turn, gathered the wisdom that is there for the asking, then as a whole we would have a lot less stress in our lives.

Jung was also of the belief that the mind was a gateway to the soul. Anxiety, he suggested, was not merely a consequence of physical survival but the evolution of the human spirit. In other words, when we take the time to learn from our life experiences, then stress offers an opportunity for spiritual growth. The mind and

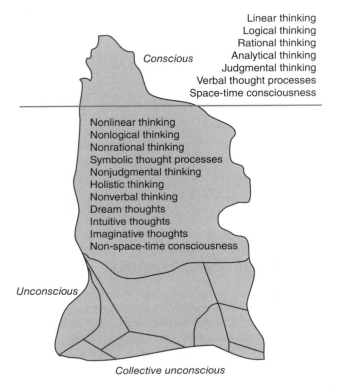

Linear thinking
Logical thinking
Rational thinking
Analytical thinking
Judgmental thinking
Verbal thought processes
Space-time consciousness

Conscious

Nonlinear thinking
Nonlogical thinking
Nonrational thinking
Symbolic thought processes
Nonjudgmental thinking
Holistic thinking
Nonverbal thinking
Dream thoughts
Intuitive thoughts
Imaginative thoughts
Non-space-time consciousness

Unconscious

Collective unconscious

Figure 2.1 An iceberg is the metaphor often used to describe the complexities of the mind, with the conscious mind (10 percent) above the water and the unconscious mind (90 percent) below; each aspect of the mind employs different thought processes.

the soul share a common space in the landscape of the human spirit. The word *psyche*, from which the word *psychology* is derived, means "soul," and it goes without saying that there is tremendous overlap between the quadrants of mental well-being and spiritual well-being. Jung was quick to note this association when he stated that every crisis over the age of 30 is a spiritual crisis. It was Jung who also noted that although we each have a personal unconscious composed of personal thoughts and memories, we are each connected to a larger reservoir of wisdom that he called the collective unconscious, where time and space play by different rules. In fact, it was a conversation with Albert Einstein about the theory of relativity that seeded the idea of the collective unconscious in Jung's mind. Much of Jung's work can be found in the roots of many stress management therapies, including dream therapy, mental imagery, and art therapy.

The Death of Expectations

Anger (fight) and fear (flight) make up the two primary stress emotions from which all other stress-related emotions derive. Over the past century, anxiety stole the spotlight, primarily because Freud thought this was the easier of the two instinctual emotions with which to work. Meanwhile anger, in all its many contemporary manifestations, began to boil over on the back burner on the world stage, from road rage and various school shootings to child and spouse abuse to international acts of terrorism to requirements to wear a face mask. First and foremost, every episode of anger, no matter how big or small, is the result of an unmet expectation. Behind every episode of anger awaits the feelings of remorse and grief.

Death is perhaps the hardest concept for the ego to reconcile. In an effort to maintain control, the ego does everything in its power to keep the upper hand. The work of Elisabeth Kübler-Ross, who observed the progression of thoughts and behaviors one experiences through one's own personal death and dying process, has now become such common knowledge that it can be found everywhere from greeting cards to cereal boxes. The stages are denial, anger, bargaining, depression, and acceptance. Grieving is a natural part of the human experience, and Kübler-Ross's stages constitute the fine art of grieving. (It should be noted that the stage after acceptance is adaptation.) Prolonged grieving, however, is not healthy and serves only to perpetuate chronic stress, yet many people never move beyond anger to acceptance, a crucial step in the resolution of all stressors.

You don't have to have terminal cancer to experience this progression of thought processes. Most likely you experience this same linear process with the death of each expectation, no matter how big or small, whether it's a dent in your new car or the breakup of your marriage. The next time you find yourself angry, ask yourself what expectation wasn't met, and therein may lie the answer to your problem.

Finding the Meaning of Life

A wise proverb is "Pain is inevitable, suffering is optional." *Suffering* is another word for stress, and chronic stress proves to be quite common with those who find themselves in an existential vacuum—a life that seems to have no purpose or meaning. Angst is a common plight among those who find themselves retired from a lifelong career, roaming an empty house made vacant by the last teenager leaving home, experiencing the sudden loss of a loved one, or even among Olympic athletes who walk off the podium with a bronze medal. Angst is also common among people who dislike their jobs. Interestingly, more heart attacks occur on Monday mornings than at any other time of the week, suggesting a link between the meaning of life and one's health. Depression, the hallmark cry of the soul, is a common malady in our stress-filled world. Despite the magic bullet of modern medicine, a chemical cure through prescribed pharmaceuticals does nothing to treat the trauma of emotional wounds. In some cases, it only masks these wounds and makes them worse by doing so.

How can suffering be optional? The voice of ageless wisdom, as echoed by Nazi concentration camp survivor, Viktor Frankl in his classic book *Man's Search for Meaning*, in which he suggests that one must create a new meaning in one's life to ease the angst of suffering. To do this, one must find a new passion, make a new goal or goals, and make a commitment to how to spend one's life energy, rather than letting it drain away. The voice of ageless wisdom advises the weary traveler to acknowledge the past but not to dwell on it. Rather, one must set one's eyes on the future, one day at a time, one step at a time, until one regains balance and can move forward on the human journey.

Energy Psychology

Perhaps because the field of psychology has worked so hard to establish its credibility as a science, it has stayed clear of all things metaphysical, including all things categorized as paranormal. However, a handful of maverick scientists and luminaries in the field of psychology have taken the initiative to integrate various aspects of ageless wisdom with many theoretical principles of modern psychology. The result forges a path to different offshoots of this discipline, starting with humanistic psychology, health psychology, and transpersonal psychology and moving on to the emerging field of **energy psychology**: a field of study that honors the mind-body-spirit dynamics and techniques to help counsel patients and clients through a wide range of psychological conditions. The premise of energy psychology is based on the ageless wisdom of the human energy matrix of subtle anatomy, including the auric field (layers of consciousness), chakras, and meridians. By using the human energy grid to detect congestion and distortions associated with mental and emotional disturbances, great gains can be made at the spiritual, mental, emotional, and physical levels to restore one to optimal health.

In the field of energy psychology, just as each layer of the auric field is associated with a specific layer of consciousness, each of the primary chakras is associated with one or more aspects of one's personality. By recognizing the various aspects of each chakra, one can begin to process and resolve issues that tend to manifest as physical symptoms. One of the techniques used in energy psychology is body tapping, also known as the emotional freedom technique (EMT), which is very similar to "energy vitamins," the means to add to or clear energy in the physical body by tapping on various meridian points.

Stress-Prone and Stress-Resistant Personalities

No topic of mental well-being would be complete without some discussion of personality types that make up the collective persona of the human species. It's fair to say that the topic of personalities is as complex as it is popular to discuss and demystify. Personality is composed of attitudes, behaviors, values, philosophies, opinions, belief systems, and perhaps much, much more. Character, a component of one's personality, is often said to be how you behave when no one else is looking. The Myers-Briggs Type Indicator, a personality type inventory based on the work of Carl Jung, is one of many personality profiles used to determine and predict how people will get along with each other. The Enneagram personality type inventory is another such tool. Perhaps because there are so many variables, personality assessments still remain more of an art than a science. Nonetheless, they offer keen insight into the complexities of the mind and how we deal with stress.

Whereas hard science points to genetic aspects (nature) that comprise aspects of one's personality, the softer sciences suggest a host of environmental factors (nurture) associated with the makeup of one's thoughts, attitudes, behaviors, and beliefs. Still others add a third dimension, ranging from astrological aspects to spiritual (karmic) considerations—all of which, to some extent, play a part in the complexities of the personality of each individual.

Although using a questionnaire to determine one's personality may be limiting, observations of character traits under stressful conditions can be quite revealing. Based on several decades of work, the following personality types have been assessed as being either stress prone or stress resistant.

Stress-Prone Personalities

People with stress-prone personalities not only do poorly in stressful situations, but with their low self-esteem, they also tend to attract more stress into their lives. Exercise 2.2 offers an assessment of possible stress-prone personality traits. The following is a list of the types:

- *Type A:* Once labeled as the impatient personality, the **Type A personality** is now regarded as someone with latent anger issues that manifest in explosive, competitive, and impetuous behaviors.
- *Type D:* New research reveals that symptoms of chronic depression (suppressed anger) may also play a primary role in coronary heart disease and perhaps other chronic illnesses. As such, Type D, like Type A, is now considered a stress personality in the category of stress-prone personalities.
- *Codependent:* This personality is composed of many traits that coalesce as a collective defense mechanism to cope with problems such as alcoholic parents or loved ones. The codependent personality is also known in rehab circles as the enabler. Approval seeking, being a super overachiever with poor boundaries, and living with a constant level of fear (primarily the fear of rejection) are common traits of this personality. Exercise 2.2 is an example of a survey to help identify traits associated with this stress-prone personality.
- *Helpless-hopeless:* This personality style best describes someone who, for whatever reason, has met failure at every turn (e.g., child abuse, sexual abuse). Self-esteem is at rock bottom, and the individual feels a lack of personal resources to help cope with problems, both big and small. Depression and feelings of helplessness and hopelessness are often associated with each other, in what sometimes can be described as a downward spiral.

Stress-Resistant Personalities

People with stress-resistant personalities tend to let small things roll off their back and deal with big problems in a very positive way. Exercise 2.3 offers an assessment of your stress-resistant personality traits. The following is a list of the types:

- *Hardy personality:* Marked by three distinct characteristics, people who exhibit the **hardy personality** demonstrate commitment to see a problem through to resolution, challenge themselves to accomplish a goal or resolve a crisis with honor, and control their emotions in a balanced way.

- *Survivor personality:* These people are true heroes who exhibit a balance of right- and left-brain skills so that problems can be approached creatively and solutions executed with confidence. Aron Ralston, a celebrated rock climber, is one example of the **survivor personality**.
- *Calculated risk taker:* This person approaches life with courage rather than fear. The **calculated risk taker** sees danger and may even thrive on it, but only after surveying all options and choosing the most level-headed approach. People who do extreme sports would fall in this category.

The evidence is quite clear that changing one's personality is impossible, yet we can begin to change our thoughts, attitudes, beliefs, and perceptions that either influence or negate various personality traits. Although you may demonstrate traits associated with the Type A or the **codependent personality**, it doesn't mean that you cannot change your thinking patterns to stop those behaviors and begin to adopt stress-resistant traits instead.

Resiliency: Getting Back Up After Being Knocked Down

The buzzword in stress management these days is *resiliency*. Resiliency is often described as the ability to bounce back from a fall. Inherent in this definition is the idea that you are bouncing back from some crisis that has knocked you down hard. It is no secret that the world today is undergoing a lot of change, from the economy and job market to healthcare issues to racial strife to dramatic climate changes that cause loss of life and property. With change comes stress, and it is no exaggeration to say that many people are getting hit hard by these changes. Simply stated, the art of resiliency is getting back up and on your feet again: standing strong. A consensus from various experts and scholars suggests that resiliency includes, but is not limited to, the following attributes: persistence, will power, optimism, flexibility, perseverance, faith, courage, patience, and adaptation. These same experts agree that everyone can become resilient, with practice. Exercise 2.5 invites you to examine your sense of resiliency.

The Power of the Mind

Holistic stress management honors the ageless wisdom of the power of the mind—the collective spirit of both conscious and unconscious minds to work in unison, as partners rather than rivals. History is punctuated with unfathomable stories of men and women who have harnessed the power of their minds to perform truly remarkable human feats. Ernest Shackleton, the captain of the *Endurance*; Rosa Parks, civil rights leader; and Aron Ralston, mountain climber, are but a few examples of people who have harnessed the power of their minds to overcome adversity. Their key to success is no secret. You, too, have the means within you to harness the power of your mind. Meditation, music therapy, visualization, mental imagery, humor therapy, and positive affirmations are a few of the many ways that the power of the mind can be disciplined and utilized not only to cope with the stress of life but also to rise to our highest human potential. Exercise 2.4 offers you a unique opportunity to begin to cultivate the power of your mind.

Chapter Summary

- According to Freud, the ego includes several defense mechanisms: denial, repression, projection, displacement, rationalization, and even humor.
- The power of two minds includes the unconscious mind, often forgotten in stress management courses. It is said that the unconscious mind controls many of our behaviors.
- Many unresolved anger issues result in prolonged grieving (the death of expectations), as explained by Elisabeth Kübler-Ross in her death and dying model, which has five stages: denial, anger, bargaining, depression, and acceptance.
- The psychology of stress includes a meaningful purpose in life, as described by Viktor Frankl. When meaning is missing, stress ensues.
- Energy psychology combines the concepts of the human energy system (e.g., chakras) with states of consciousness and the resolution of stress.
- Some people seem prone to stress, whereas others seem to be immune from it. The concept of stress-prone and stress-resistant personalities invites us to examine our personality and to change behaviors that promote stress while enhancing factors that resist it.

Additional Resources

Beattie, M. *Codependent No More*. Center City, MN: Hazelden; 2013.

Bernstein, A. *The Myth of Stress*. New York: Simon & Schuster; 2010.

Craig, G. *The EFT Manual: Emotional Freedom Technique*, 2nd ed. Fulton, CA: Energy Psychology Press; 2011.

Eden, D. *Energy Medicine*. New York: Tarcher/Putnam; 2008.

Frankl, V. *Man's Search for Meaning*. New York: Ebury Publishing; 1959, 2000, 2013.

Hanson, R. *Resilient: How to Grow an Unshakable Core of Calm, Strength and Happiness*. New York: Harmony Books; 2018.

Kübler-Ross, E. *On Death and Dying*, rev. ed. New York: Scribner; 2014.

Miller, M. C. The Dangers of Chronic Distress. *Newsweek*. October 3, 2005, pp. 58–59.

Peirce, P. *Frequency: The Power of Personal Vibration*. New York: Atria; 2011.

Seligman, M. *Authentic Happiness*. New York: Free Press; 2002.

Shackleton, E. *South: The Last Antarctic Expedition of Shackleton and the Endurance*. New York: Lyons Press; 1919, 2008.

Siebert, A. *The Resiliency Advantage*. San Francisco, CA: Berrett-Koehler Publishers; 2005.

Siebert, A. *The Survivor Personality*. New York: Perigee; 2010.

CHAPTER 3

Stress and the Body

KEY TERMS

Chakra
Human energy field
Immune system–related disorders
Meridians
Microbiome

Nervous system–related disorders
Self-healing
Subtle anatomy
Well-being

Here is a startling statistic: More than 80 percent of patients' visits to physicians' offices are associated with stress (unresolved issues of anger and fear). Moreover, 80 percent of workers' compensation claims are directly related to stress. Here is another statistic: Researchers in the field of psychoneuroimmunology (PNI) and energy healing suggest that as much as 85 percent of illness and disease is associated with stress, and they also note a direct causal link, providing a new perspective on the word *disease*. Anyone who has ever suffered a tension headache knows intuitively how strong the mind-body connection is.

Rest assured that the dynamics of disease and illness are quite complex and yet to be fully understood. This chapter combines the best aspects of both Western and Eastern wisdom for a more comprehensive understanding of mind-body-spirit health and well-being.

Today, it is well documented that stress aggravates several health conditions, particularly type 2 diabetes, eczema, and rheumatoid arthritis. Furthermore, many diseases, such as lupus, fibromyalgia, Epstein-Barr virus, rheumatoid arthritis, and type 1 diabetes, are now thought to have an autoimmune component to them. The list of stress-related illnesses continues to grow, from herpes and hemorrhoids to the common cold, cancer, and practically everything in between. Pharmaceuticals and surgery are the two tools of the trade used in Western (allopathic) medicine, yet the trade-offs can include severe side effects. This is one reason why so many people are turning to complementary forms of integrative healing for chronic health problems.

Prior to the discovery of vaccinations and antibiotics, the leading cause of death was infectious diseases. Today the leading causes of death are chronic lifestyle diseases (e.g., most cancer, diabetes, obesity, stroke, coronary heart disease), all of which have a strong stress component to them. Moreover, an increasing number of people suffer from chronic pain that ranges from bothersome discomfort to complete immobility. The Western model of health care (which some people call "sick care") places a strong focus on symptomatic relief rather than prevention and healing restoration. As we are now learning, the most advantageous approach appears to combine the best of allopathic and holistic healing to address both the causes and symptoms of stress that will return one back to homeostasis, turning the battleground into a peaceful landscape. Exercise 3.1 is a personal stress inventory to help you determine any association between stress and symptoms of stress in your body.

Stress and Chronic Pain

In addition to issues related to chronic disease, an increasing number of Americans suffer from debilitating chronic pain. Muscular pain associated with the lower back, hips, shoulders, and neck can be a constant nightmare, so much so that it steals your attention from practically everything else. The connection between stress and chronic pain cannot be ignored. (Neither can the connection between stress and obesity.) All of these factors are tightly integrated. It may come as no surprise that many of the coping and relaxation techniques in the cadre of holistic stress management used to maintain health and **well-being** are well documented as a means to help restore a sense of homeostasis as well.

Stress and Inflammation

Researchers in the field of PNI have now discovered that chronic stress is associated with the body's inability to regulate the inflammatory response. This inability, due in part to the role cortisol has on the immune system, appears to be a strong link in the stress and chronic disease equation. Sheldon Cohen, a researcher at Carnegie Mellon University, found that people with high levels of inflammation (chronic inflammation) were more susceptible to colds and flu. Further research from the Oral Biology lab at Ohio State University reveals that chronic stress, due to repeated firing of the sympathetic nervous system, appears to change the gene activity of immune cells before they enter the bloodstream. Inflammation, now confirmed to be a result of stress, is associated with many chronic diseases and the acceleration of the aging process and is tied to both the nervous system and the immune system. Inflammation and the pain that results from it are also associated with the use of pain relievers and the opioid epidemic. The association between stress and inflammation highlights just one of many mind–body connections.

Your Human Space Suit

Renowned inventor and philosopher Buckminster Fuller once said that the human body is our one and only space suit in which to inhabit Spaceship Earth. It comes with its own oxygen tank, a metabolic waste removal system, a sensory detector system to enjoy all the pleasures of planetary exploration, and an immune defense system to ensure the health of the space suit in the occasionally harsh global environment. This specially designed space suit also is equipped with a unique program for self-healing. Factors associated with this self-healing process include the basic common health behaviors associated with longevity: regular physical exercise, proper nutrition, adequate sleep, the avoidance of drugs, and a supportive community of friends and family. Unfortunately, most people do not take good care of their space suits, and many have forgotten the means to activate the program for self-healing.

Fight-or-Flight with a Bite

The fight-or-flight response may begin with a perception in the mind, but this thought process quickly becomes a series of neurological and chemical reactions in the body. In the blink of an eye, the nervous system releases epinephrine and norepinephrine throughout the body for immediate blood redistribution and muscle contraction. At the same time, a flood of hormones prepares the body for immediate and long-term metabolic survival. Similar to the cascade of a waterfall, hormones are secreted from the brain's pituitary and hypothalamus glands to serve as messengers moving quickly downstream to the adrenal glands (cone-shaped organs, one of which sits atop each kidney). Upon neural command, cortisol, aldosterone, and other glucocorticoids infiltrate the bloodstream to do their jobs, all in the name of physical survival.

What works well for acute stress can cause serious problems with chronic stress. Repeated synthesis and release of these stress hormones day after day (the consequence of prolonged bouts of unresolved stress issues) can literally wreak havoc on the physical body. In essence, the body becomes the battlefield for the war games of the mind.

Physiology of Stress: The Neural/ Hormonal Pathways of Stress and Relaxation

Your nervous system is comprised of both a sympathetic (stress) and parasympathetic (relaxation) tract. The sympathetic nervous system secretes the catecholamines epinephrine and norepinephrine. These two substances are released at the onset of the stress (fight-or-flight) response via the neural endings in order to get you to move by increasing heart rate, blood pressure, and so on. Through a complex series of neurochemical reactions under stress (from the pituitary and hypothalamus to the adrenal glands), the body prepares for survival. Many hormones are secreted throughout the initial and subsequent reactions to stress, but the hormone most closely associated with the stress response is cortisol, commonly known as the *stress hormone*. Other pathways involving hormones (e.g., thyroxine) for chronic stress also come into play. The parasympathetic nervous system secretes acetylcholine, a substance used to return the body, after being stressed, to homeostasis, a state we all need to be in more often.

DNA, Telomeres, Stress, and Aging

At both ends of each DNA strand is a region of repetitive sequences that serves to protect the end of the chromosome from deterioration. These telomeres are associated with DNA replication and become shorter each time the process is repeated. The enzyme telomerase is used to protect the telomeres by ensuring their stability. If the telomeres shorten without restoration, then cell replication is compromised. When cell replication is compromised, tissue health is compromised, as seen in the aging process. In 2009, the Nobel Prize in Medicine was awarded to researchers whose work substantiated the importance of telomeres. Research now substantiates the fact that oxidative stress (free radicals) shortens telomeres; hence, this type of stress compromises health in a number of ways, including cell division and the integrity of our DNA. Speculation is that chronic stress may also have the same effect.

Physical exercise is suggested as a means to enhance the integrity of the telomeres. Do other relaxation techniques also lead to the fountain of youth? Perhaps! Although more research is needed, all evidence points in this direction. Stress not only kills but also speeds up the aging process.

The Human Microbiome: A Look at Health Through the Gut

One of the newest discoveries related to disease and illness is not found in viruses or even deep inside the strands of your DNA but within millions upon millions of bacteria that reside in your stomach and small intestine. Researchers now call the intestinal flora, comprised of trillions of healthy bacteria, the **microbiome**. We host a vast and diverse living ecological system within us. When this ecological system is healthy, so are we. When it is compromised, so are we. The 20th-century approach of wiping out "bugs" via antibiotics has led to a "deforestation" of essential bacteria. The end result sets the stage for chronic illness of many kinds. Maintaining the integrity of the microbiome, however, is far more complicated than eating yogurt or consuming probiotics to reseed the forest of your intestinal flora.

It is now known that 70 percent of our immune system resides in the gut, yet the gut is often ignored in the treatment of many chronic diseases, from asthma, obesity, and arthritis to multiple sclerosis, psoriasis, and attention-deficit/hyperactivity disorder (ADHD). Perhaps the biggest take-home message about a compromised microbiome is the association between it and inflammation. Inflammation (excessive oxidation of tissues) is associated with a great many chronic diseases, and stress seems to be a major trigger resulting in inflammation. Moreover, abysmal eating habits perpetuate a compromised microbiome, leaving one quite vulnerable to chronic disease.

Gross Anatomy and Physiology

Your body is composed of a network of several amazing systems that work together as an alliance for the necessary functions of all daily life activities. For centuries, these aspects were identified as nine separate systems living under the anatomical structure of the human body. Now most health experts agree (through the wisdom of PNI) that this is truly one system, with the whole always being greater than the sum of the parts. The parts are the musculoskeletal system, nervous system, cardiovascular system, pulmonary system, endocrine system, reproductive system, renal system, digestive system, and immune system. If you initially have a health problem with one of these systems, eventually all other systems become directly affected. Physical well-being is often described as the optimal functioning of all of these physiological systems. In union with this "one system" are the many anatomical organs responsible for the integrity of its work, including, but not limited to, the heart, lungs, kidneys, liver, stomach, pancreas, brain, and lymph nodes.

What comes to mind when you hear the expression "the picture of health"? For most people this conjures an image of a physically fit person enjoying some rigorous outdoor activity well into their later years. Sadly, this has now become an image to which few can relate. Stress not only can affect the optimal functioning of all of these physiological systems to destroy the picture of health, but it also can literally shut down the entire body. Simply stated: Left unresolved, stress kills! Exercise 3.2 is a questionnaire that brings to your attention the health habits that make a composite of your current health picture.

Subtle Anatomy and Physiology

Equally important, yet often less obvious than gross anatomy, are three other systems critical to the operations of the human space suit. These are more commonly known as **subtle anatomy** and physiology, and they are the human energy field, the meridian system, and the chakra system. A holistic perspective of health would be incomplete without mentioning this aspect of health. The following sections provide a more detailed look at the aspects of our subtle anatomy and physiology.

The Human Energy Field

Western science has recently discovered that the human body has a unique field of electromagnetic energy that not only surrounds but also permeates the entire body. This **human energy field**, which mystics often call the *human aura*, is the basis of Kirlian photography and the diagnosis of disease through magnetic resonance imaging (MRI). Ageless wisdom notes that there are many layers of the human energy field, with each layer associated with some aspect of consciousness (e.g., instinct, intellect, intuition, emotions). This and other findings support the timeless premise that our mind isn't located in our body. Instead, our body is located in our mind!

Each layer of consciousness in the human energy field is considered a harmonic vibration. Like the keys of a piano keyboard, the frequency of the body's vibrations, and that of the emotional, mental, and spiritual fields, is set at different octaves, yet all are within the harmonic range of each other. If a thought coupled with an emotion is left unresolved, it can cause dissonance or imbalance within the layers of energy in the aura. Distortion first appears in the aura outside the physical body. When left unresolved, these emotional frequencies cascade through the layers of energy (which include the chakras and meridians) to pool within various cell tissues. The end result is dysfunction in the corresponding area in the physical body. Dissonance (the opposite of resonance) eventually appears at the cellular level, and the once harmonic vibration is no longer tuned to homeostasis, hence setting the stage for disease and illness. Medical intuitives—including Mona Lisa Schulz, MD; Judith Orloff, MD; Caroline Myss; Donna Eden; Mietek Wirkus; and others— describe the initial stage of illness and disease as unresolved emotions (e.g., anger or fear). Through this model of well-being, disease develops outside the body and filters down through the layers of energy. Ironically, physical symptoms in the body are not the first signs of illness but, rather, the last. The body indeed becomes the battlefield for the war games of the mind.

The Meridian System

First brought to the world's attention through ancient Chinese culture, the physical body holds 12 bilateral rivers (**meridians**) of energy or *chi*. Each meridian connects to one or more vital organs (e.g., heart, lungs, liver, kidneys). When energy is blocked or congested in any meridian, the health of the associated organ will suffer. Acupuncture, the primary modality used to ensure the free flow of energy through these meridians, uses placement of tiny bulblike needles at various gates (acupuncture points) along the meridian pathways to unblock energy congestion. Acupressure (also known as *shiatsu*) is another method used for energy regulation. Although Western medicine doesn't quite acknowledge the concept of chi or meridians, it does recognize many remarkable outcomes of acupuncture (without side effects) in the treatment of chronic illnesses for which Western medicine itself has proven less than effective.

The Chakra Energy System

The human body is said to have seven major energy portals. The ancient Sanskrit word for these energy portals is **chakra**, which translates as "spinning wheel" and looks like a small tornado of energy attached to the body. Like the meridian energy system, each chakra is associated with the health of vital organs specific to the region to which it's attached. When the chakra shows signs of congestion or distortion, then the life force of energy through the chakra cannot be maintained in its specific region and the health of those organs is compromised. Each chakra is associated not only with a body region but also with a layer of consciousness in the human energy field, directly linking mind, body, and spirit. Exercise 3.3 explores the concept of chakras and your health status.

The science behind subtle energy provides valuable insight into a problem that has vexed Western health experts who study stress and disease: Why is it that two people who go through a similar stressful experience can contract different chronic illnesses? The answer may appear to be strongly associated with the dynamics of the chakra energy system. The following is a brief summary of the seven primary chakras.

First Chakra

The first chakra is commonly known as the root chakra and is located at the base of the spine. The root chakra is associated with issues of safety and security. It also has a relationship with our connectedness to the earth and feelings of groundedness. The root chakra is tied energetically to some organs of the reproductive system as well as the hip joints, lower back, and pelvic area. Health problems in these areas, including lower back pain, sciatica, rectal difficulties, and some cancers (e.g., prostate), are thought to correspond to disturbances of the root chakra. The root chakra is also known as the seat of the Kundalini energy, a spiritually based concept yet to be understood in Western culture.

Second Chakra

The second chakra, also known as the sacral chakra, is associated with the sex organs as well as personal power related to business and social relationships. The second chakra deals with emotions associated with sexuality and self-worth. Self-worth viewed through external means, such as money, job, or sexuality, causes an energy distortion in this chakra region. Obsessiveness with material gain is thought to be a means to compensate for low self-worth; hence, it distorts this chakra. Common symptoms associated with this chakra region may include menstrual difficulties, infertility, vaginal infections, ovarian cysts, impotency, lower back pain, prostate problems, sexual dysfunction, slipped disks, and bladder and urinary infections.

Third Chakra

Located in the upper stomach region, the third chakra is also known as the solar plexus chakra. Energetically, this chakra feeds into the organs of the GI tract, including the abdomen, small intestine, colon, gallbladder, kidneys, liver, pancreas, adrenal glands, and spleen. Not to be confused with self-worth, the region of the third chakra is associated with self-confidence, self-respect, and empowerment. The wisdom of the solar plexus chakra is more commonly known as a gut feeling, an intuitive sense closely tied to our level of personal power, as exemplified in the expression "This doesn't feel right." Blockages to this chakra are thought to be related to ulcers, cancerous tumors, diabetes, hepatitis, anorexia, bulimia, and all stomach-related problems. Issues of unresolved anger and fear are deeply connected to organic dysfunction in this body region.

Fourth Chakra

The fourth chakra is affectionately known as the heart chakra, and it is considered to be one of the most important energy centers of the body. The heart chakra represents the ability to express love. Like a symbolic heart placed over the organic heart, feelings of unresolved anger or expressions of conditional love work to congest the heart chakra, which in turn has a corresponding effect on the anatomical heart, as noted by renowned cardiologist Dean Ornish. The heart, however, is not the only organ closely tied to the heart chakra. Other organs include the lungs, breasts, and esophagus. Symptoms of a blocked heart chakra can include heart attacks, enlarged heart, asthma, allergies, lung cancer, bronchial difficulties, circulation problems, breast cancer, and problems associated with the upper back and shoulders. An important association also exists between the heart chakra and the thymus gland. The thymus gland, so instrumental in the making of T cells, which are central to the immune response, shrinks with age.

Fifth Chakra

The fifth chakra lies above and is connected to the throat. Organs associated with the throat chakra are the thyroid and parathyroid glands, mouth, vocal cords, and trachea. As a symbol of communication, the throat chakra represents the development of personal expression, creativity, purpose in life, and willpower. The inability to express feelings or creativity or to exercise one's will freely inevitably distort the flow of energy to the throat chakra and is thought to result in chronic sore throat problems, temporomandibular joint dysfunction (TMJD), mouth sores, stiffness in the neck area, thyroid dysfunction, migraines, and even cancerous tumors in this region.

Sixth Chakra

The sixth chakra is more commonly known as the brow chakra or the third eye. This chakra is associated with intuition and the ability to access the ageless wisdom or bank of knowledge in the depths of universal consciousness. As energy moves through the dimension of universal wisdom into this chakra, it promotes the development of intelligence and reasoning skills. Directly tied to the pituitary and pineal glands, this chakra feeds energy to the brain for information processing. Unlike the solar plexus chakra, which is responsible for a gut level of intuition with personal matters, the wisdom channeled through the brow chakra is more universal in nature with implications for the spiritual aspect of life. Diseases caused by dysfunction of the brow chakra (e.g., brain tumors, hemorrhages, blood clots, blindness, comas, depression, schizophrenia) may be caused by not wanting to see something that is extremely important to one's soul growth.

Seventh Chakra

If the concept of chakras is foreign to the Western mind, then the seventh chakra may hold promise to bridge East and West. Featured most predominantly in the Judeo-Christian culture through paintings and sculptures as the halo over holy persons and saintly beings, the seventh chakra, also known as the crown chakra, is associated with matters of the soul and the spiritual quest. When the crown chakra is open and fully functioning, it is known to access the highest level of consciousness. Although no specific disease or illness may be associated with the crown chakra, in truth every disease has a spiritual significance.

Although not everyone can see or sense the human energy field, meridians, or chakras, you can be trained to do so. Exercise 3.4, "Energy Ball Exercise," is an introduction to the perceptions of the human energy field. Exercise 3.5 includes several ideas for maintaining a healthy flow of personal energy or chi.

Stress and the Immune System

It's no surprise to learn that the immune system is greatly compromised under chronic stress, beginning with the immunoglobulins in the saliva down to the natural killer cells that scan the body for unwanted pathogens and mutant cancer cells. Chances are if you were to look back to the most recent time you became ill, right before it (days, even weeks) you'll find a stressful experience that triggered a cascade of unresolved stress emotions, in turn washing a flood of stress hormones through your body.

What physiological factors are responsible for a suppressed immune system? At first, the central nervous system (e.g., epinephrine, norepinephrine) was implicated. Attention soon turned to cortisol, the stress hormone secreted by the adrenal glands and responsible for a host of metabolic survival activities. Apparently, when cortisol gets done with its fight-or-flight duties, for some unknown reason it has a nasty habit of attacking and destroying white blood cells, which comprise the front-line defense of the immune system. Research suggests that cortisol is not the only culprit when it comes to an immune system compromised by stress. Landmark research by Candace Pert and others determined that various neuropeptides, secreted by the brain and other cells in the body, are triggered by emotional responses. Pert calls these "molecules of emotion," and they can either enhance or detract from the efficacy of the immune system. In essence, thoughts are energy—they can kill or heal.

Recently, a significant discovery was made linking the brain to the immune system, revealing a distinct connection among our thoughts, emotions, and health. The connection between the brain and lymphatic system is through the meningeal lymphatic vessels, cites Antoine Louveau, researcher at the University of Virginia School of Medicine's Department of Neuroscience.

Through the lens of holistic wellness, it is important to realize that the immune system does not reside solely in the body. The aspects that comprise your subtle anatomy also constitute your immune system.

The Stress and Disease Connection

Through the eyes of Western science, which views each human being as a machine, stress is often described as "wear and tear" on the physical body. Like a car that has covered more than 200,000 miles, the body has parts that typically break down and need to be fixed or replaced.

In this paradigm, these parts are often called target organs because they seem to be specifically targeted by neurochemical pathways produced by chronic stress. Any organ can be a target organ: hair, skin, blood vessels, joints, muscles, stomach, colon, and others. In some people one organ may be targeted, whereas in others many organs can be affected. First, we'll take a look at disease and illness from a Western perspective and then conclude with a holistic view of the healing system. Western science classifies stress-related disorders into two categories: **nervous system–related disorders** and **immune system–related disorders**. The following is a brief listing of chronic diseases from each of these two categories.

Nervous System-Related Disorders

- *Tension headaches:* Tension headaches are produced by contractions of the muscles of the forehead, eyes, neck, and jaw. Increased pain results from increased contraction of these muscles. Lower back pain can also result from the same process. Although pain relievers such as ibuprofen (Advil) are the most common sources of relief, tension headaches have also been shown to dissipate with the use of meditation, mental imagery, and biofeedback.
- *Migraine headaches:* A migraine headache is a vascular headache. Symptoms can include a flash of light followed by intense throbbing, dizziness, and nausea. Migraines are thought to be related to the inability to express anger and frustration. Although several medications are prescribed for migraines, biofeedback, mental imagery, and the herb feverfew can be equally effective and used with fewer side effects.
- *TMJD:* Excessive contraction of the jaw muscles can lead to TMJD. In many cases, people are unaware that they have this dysfunction because the behavioral

damage (grinding one's teeth) occurs during sleep. Like migraines, TMJD is often associated with the inability to express feelings of anger. Relaxation techniques, including biofeedback and progressive muscular relaxation, have been shown to be effective in decreasing the muscular tension associated with TMJD.

- *Bronchial asthma:* In this illness, a pronounced secretion of bronchial fluids causes a swelling of the smooth muscle tissue of the large air passageways (bronchi). The onset of asthmatic attacks is often associated with anxiety. Currently drugs (e.g., prednisone) are the first method of treatment. However, relaxation techniques, including mental imagery, autogenic training, and meditation, may be just as effective in both delaying the onset and reducing the severity of these attacks.

- *Irritable bowel syndrome (IBS):* IBS is characterized by repeated bouts of abdominal pain or tenderness, cramps, diarrhea, nausea, constipation, and excessive flatulence. One reason IBS is considered so directly related to stress is that the hypothalamus, which controls appetite regulation (hunger and satiety), is also closely associated with emotional regulation. Relaxation skills, including thermal biofeedback, progressive muscular relaxation, mental imagery, and reframing, can help to reduce existing levels of anxiety with promising results.

- *Coronary heart disease (CHD):* Elevated blood pressure (hypertension) is a significant risk factor for CHD. Stress hormones are often responsible for increasing blood pressure. When pressure is increased in a closed system, the risk of damage to vascular tissue due to increased turbulence is significantly increased. This damage to the vessel walls appears as small microtears, particularly in the intima lining of the coronary heart vessels, which supply the heart muscle (myocardium) with oxygen. As a way of healing these tears, several constituents floating in the blood bind with the damaged vascular cell tissue. Paradoxically, the primary "healing" agent is cholesterol, a sticky substance found floating in the blood serum whose buildup can result in atherosclerosis, which can eventually lead to a heart attack.

Immune System-Related Disorders

- *Common cold and influenza:* Stress hormones (specifically cortisol) tend to destroy members of the white blood cell family, suppressing the immune system, hence leaving a person susceptible to cold and flu.

- *Allergies:* An allergic reaction is initiated when a foreign substance (e.g., pollen, dust spores) enters the body. However, in some people, allergic reactions can occur just by thinking about a stimulus that provoked a previous attack. Allergic reactions are also more prevalent and severe in people who are prone to anxiety. Over-the-counter medications containing antihistamines and allergy shots (injections) are the most common approaches to dealing with allergies. Relaxation techniques also help minimize the effects of allergy-promoting substances.

- *Rheumatoid arthritis:* This joint and connective tissue disease occurs when synovial membrane tissue swells, causing the joint to become inflamed. In time, synovial fluid may enter cartilage and bone tissue, causing further deterioration of the affected joint(s). The severity of arthritic pain is often related to episodes of stress, particularly suppressed anger. The treatment for this disease varies from pain relievers (e.g., ibuprofen) to steroid injections (e.g., cortisone), depending on the severity of pain and the rate of joint deterioration. Relaxation techniques offer a complementary modality to help reduce these symptoms.

- *Ulcers and colitis:* More than 75 percent of ulcers are caused by *Helicobacter* bacteria, which create an open wound that stomach acids only worsen. Treatment with antibiotics is now shown to be highly effective for a large percentage of people who have ulcers, yet two questions remain: What makes some people more vulnerable to *Helicobacter* than others? Why are antibiotics effective in only 75 percent of the cases of people with ulcers? Stress is thought to be the answer.

- *Cancer:* Cancer has been proven to be one of the most perplexing diseases of our time, affecting one in every three Americans. The body typically produces an abnormal cell once every 6 hours, but the natural killer cells of the immune system roam the body to search for and destroy these mutant cells. Stress hormones tend to suppress the immune system, allowing some mutant cells to become cancerous tumors. The treatments for cancer include chemotherapy, radiation, and surgery. However, coping skills involving cognitive restructuring, art therapy, and relaxation techniques including mental imagery and meditation are being used as complementary healing methods. Although in themselves these methods are not a cure for cancer, in some cases they seem to have a pronounced effect when used in combination with traditional medicine.

The Dynamics of Self-Healing

All things being equal, the body craves homeostasis and will do all it can to maintain a sense of balance. The body has a remarkable ability to heal itself when given the chance to do so. Exercise, nutrition, and sleep play essential roles in the healing process, but so do our thoughts and feelings. Ultimately, disease, in all its many forms, is a sign that something is clearly out of balance among mind, body, and spirit. Chronic illness suggests that the body's attempt to regain that inner balance is compromised, most likely by lifestyle behaviors that don't support the healing process.

In his acclaimed book *Spontaneous Healing*, Dr. Andrew Weil documents the unique **self-healing** processes of the human body, from the body's wisdom to kill germs by raising the body's core temperature to the role of a specific enzyme to repair DNA. Deepak Chopra approaches the topic in a similar way in his book *Quantum Healing*. For instance, Chopra explains that every cell in the body regenerates itself; some regenerate within a matter of days, others take years. The life span of red blood cells, for instance, is approximately 37 days. Nerve cells seem to take the longest. We know now that even brain cells have the capacity to regenerate. Consequently, within a 7-year time period, every person has a completely new body of cells.

Most cancerous tumors take years, even decades, to grow. So why is it, then, that with a new body we have old tumors? Perhaps the answer resides in the vibrations of consciousness that surround and permeate each and every cell and that get passed on from generation to generation of cells through a process called entrainment. *Entrainment* is a physics term used to describe sympathetic resonance between two objects. It's commonly known in physics circles as the law of conservation of energy. A classic example of human entrainment is observed when women who live or work together begin to see a synchronization of their menstrual periods. Where there are neighboring energies, there is entrainment as well. Every cell vibrates with energy, as do tumors.

Unlike conventional wisdom, which states that only brain cells hold some level of consciousness, it now appears that every cell in the body contains a vibration of consciousness. It is suggested that this imprint of conscious frequency is then transferred via entrainment from cell to cell, thus allowing a tumor to develop and keep growing, long after the original aberrant cells have died off.

Can changes in one's thoughts change the vibration of cells? The answer appears to be yes, in a critical mass of people—those who demonstrate "spontaneous remission" of cancerous tumors.

Which emotions are prone to compromise the integrity of the immune system? In simplest terms, any lingering unresolved emotion associates with the fight-or-flight response. It would be too hard to single out anger and fear as the only culprits; however, both of these serve as umbrella emotions for literally hundreds of other emotions, which along with joy, love, and happiness constitute the full spectrum of feelings. As mentioned, none of these emotions are bad when used properly, not even anger or fear. However, when left unresolved, anger or fear and all the many ways in which these two survival emotions manifest will, over time, suppress the immune system. In doing so, they open the door wide to a multitude of health-related problems.

Just as a preponderance of unhealthy emotions can suppress the immune system, positive thoughts and feelings can enhance it. Although all aspects of the inherent self-healing program are not fully understood, one thing is clear: Effective coping skills that help to resolve the causes of stress in tandem with effective relaxation skills that strive to return the body to homeostasis offer the best opportunity to engage the healing process to its fullest potential.

Chapter Summary

- An extended stress response beyond "physical survival" creates wear and tear on many physiological systems of the human body, including the cardiovascular, digestive, and endocrine systems.
- Just as there is gross anatomy, there is also subtle anatomy—specifically, the human energy field and the meridian and chakra systems, all of which are connected to the mind-body-spirit continuum.
- Prolonged (chronic) stress definitely has an impact on the immune system—in essence, suppressing it and thus making a person more vulnerable to disease and illness.
- The stress and disease connection is very real. Chronic stress is now related to a number of health-related problems ranging from the common cold to cancer.
- The body actually needs some stress (e.g., exercise), but it also craves homeostasis. Many, if not all, stress management techniques promote self-healing dynamics by helping the body return to homeostasis.

Additional Resources

APA Online. Stress Affects Immunity in Ways Related to Stress Type and Duration, as Shown by Nearly 300 Studies. 2004. *Media Information*. https://www.apa.org/news/press/releases/2004/07/stress-immune. Accessed November 8, 2020.

Arntz, W., Chasse, B., & Vicente, M. *What the Bleep Do We Know!?* Deerfield Beach, FL: Health Communications; 2005.

Barney, J. They'll Have to Rewrite the Textbooks. March 21, 2016. *UVA Today*. https://news.virginia.edu/illimitable/discovery/theyll-have-rewrite-textbooks. Accessed November 8, 2020.

Blackburn, E., & Epel, E. *The Telomere Effect*. New York, NY: Grand Central Publishing; 2017.

Chiasson, A. M. *Energy Healing: The Essentials of Self-Care*. Boulder, CO: Sounds True; 2013.

Chopra, D. *Quantum Healing*. New York, NY: Bantam; 1990.

Dale, C. *The Subtle Body: An Encyclopedia of Your Energetic Body*. Boulder, CO: Sounds True; 2009.

Dispenza, J. *Evolve Your Brain: The Science of Changing Your Mind*. Deerfield Beach, FL: Health Communications; 2007.

Eden, D. *Energy Medicine*. New York, NY: Tarcher/Putnam; 2008.

Gerber, R. *Vibrational Medicine*, 3rd ed. Rochester, VT: Bear & Company; 2001.

Lipton, B. *The Biology of Belief: Unleashing the Power of Consciousness, Matter, and Miracles*. Santa Rosa, CA: Mountain of Love/Elite; 2008.

Louveau, A., Smirnov, I., Keyes, T., et al. Structural and Functional Features of Central Nervous System Lymphatic Vessels. *Nature* 523:337–341. June 1, 2015. https://www.nature.com/articles/nature14432. Accessed November 8, 2020.

Mate, G. *When the Body Says No: Exploring the Stress and Disease Connection*. New York, NY: Wiley; 2011.

McTaggart, L. *The Field*. New York, NY: HarperCollins; 2008.

Ornish, D. *Love and Survival*. New York, NY: HarperCollins; 1998.

Pelletier, K. *Change Your Genes, Change Your Life*. San Rafael, CA: Origin Press; 2019.

Pert, C. *Molecules of Emotion*. New York, NY: Scribner; 1997.

Powell, D., & Institute of Noetic Sciences. *The 2007 Shift Report: Evidence of a World Transforming*. Petaluma, CA: Institute of Noetic Sciences; 2007, pp. 28–36.

Segerstrom, S. C., & Miller, G. E. Psychological Stress and the Human Immune System: A Meta-Analytical Study of 30 Years of Inquiry. *Psychological Bulletin* 130(4):601–630, 2004.

Swanson, C. *Life Force: The Scientific Basis*, 2nd ed. Tucson, AZ: Poseidia Press; 2009.

Weil, A. *Spontaneous Healing*. New York, NY: Knopf; 2000.

Effective Coping Skills

CHAPTER 4

Positive Mind-Set

KEY TERM

Toxic thoughts

The Ageless Wisdom of Positive Thinking

There are those who say the world is composed of two kinds of people: optimists and pessimists. Ageless wisdom reveals that within the mind of each person there are at least two voices—a positive and a negative influence—suggesting that each of us contains the potential for both mind-sets. Since the days of Plato and perhaps much earlier, it has been observed that the direction of one's life, by and large, is a product of one's thoughts and attitudes. To be sure, we cannot avoid life's problems; however, our attitude about each situation tends to reveal the outcome. Changing one's attitude provides the impetus to change the direction of one's life. As the old adage goes, "Attitude is the paintbrush with which we paint the world." During the first 11 months of the COVID pandemic, many people complained about their favorite restaurants, gyms, and movie theaters that had closed, cancelled weddings and summer concerts and sporting events, and having to wear face masks everywhere. Yet this time of the "great reset" also gave many people pause for thought. Memes posted on social media reinforced a shift in thinking with phrases like these: "You are not stuck at home—you are safe at home: Enjoy the difference." and "A face mask is a lot more comfortable than a respirator." Likewise, many people began to shift their thinking from victimization to gratitude for what they had.

In his critically acclaimed book *Man's Search for Meaning*, Viktor Frankl credited his survival in the most notorious Nazi concentration camp, Auschwitz, to his ability to find meaning in his suffering, a meaning that strengthened his willpower and choice of attitude. Frankl noted that despite the fact that prisoners were stripped of all their possessions and many essential human rights, the one thing concentration camp officials could not take away was their ability to choose the perceptions of their circumstances. To quote another adage, "Each situation has a good side and a bad side. Each moment, you decide."

If you listen to the news much these days, you might notice several references to the Great Depression with regard to the economy. As it turns out, the period of the Great Depression was about the economy but also psychology. Although many people struggled day by day, some people thrived in the face of adversity. We see that same dichotomy emerge again in our current troubled economic times.

The phrase *self-fulfilling prophecy* was used long before Freud coined the word *ego*. Ageless wisdom confirms the idea that negative thoughts tend to create and often perpetuate negative circumstances, and positive thoughts tend to perpetuate positive circumstances. Current research regarding the power of intention upholds this wisdom. Our thoughts, attitudes, perceptions, and beliefs unite as a powerful source of conscious energy. Therefore, it makes sense to use this energy in the best way possible.

The Influence of the Media

Current estimates suggest that the average person is bombarded with more than 3,000 advertisements a day from television, radio, T-shirts, billboards, and the Internet— all of which constantly inundate us with messages that strike at our insecurities. In marketing circles this is known as aggressive, in-your-face tactics. The desired result leaves you with an underlying sense of inadequacy, if not an inferiority complex. There is no doubt this method works, otherwise marketers would move on to a different strategy. Likewise, constant scrolling on social media lends itself to lifestyle comparisons, philosophical comparisons, and a lot of self-judgment.

Corporate marketing is only part of the fear-based media equation. As was so poignantly illustrated in the 2002 Academy Award-winning documentary *Bowling for Columbine*, both local and national news broadcasts have discovered that the addictive nature of fear sells. Even the Weather Channel has changed its focus to broadcast weather-related disasters between forecast updates in order to keep viewers' attention. Even the federal government was accused of using the media to fan the flames of anxiety with hypervigilant color-coded terrorism alerts. One of the best ways to increase your tolerance of negative media is to reduce your exposure to it, limiting the time you spend watching television and social media, if not stopping altogether.

An Attitude of Gratitude

Although it's true that it is difficult, if not impossible, to give sincere thanks for a crisis at the moment it appears (that's called denial), continuously dwelling on a problem tends to make things worse. A shift in consciousness toward what are blessings tends to balance the negative thoughts that persist from personal stressors. In doing so, an attitude of gratitude provides a perspective that helps resolve the problem at hand. In the midst of stress, regardless of the size of the problem, it is easy to take things for granted.

The preferred option is to count your blessings by seeing even the smallest things as gifts. One aspect of reframing suggests to do just that: adopt an attitude of gratitude for all the things in your life that are going right, rather than curse all the things that seem to be going wrong. In a society where only 1 day out of 365 is dedicated to giving thanks, the regular practice of an attitude of gratitude may not frequently be encouraged. But remember: This is the same society that promotes fear-based television programming. Buck the tide and make a habit of giving thanks regularly.

In hindsight, what appears to be a curse may actually be looked upon as a blessing. Many people caught in the midst of a crisis utter "This is the worst thing that ever happened to me," only to reframe this perspective later as "This was the best thing that ever happened to me."

The Art of Acceptance

Clearly, some things in life we cannot change, nor can we change the people involved in these situations. Attempting to do so becomes a series of control dramas that only perpetuate the cycles of stress. The ability to accept a situation for what it is, rather than exerting (and wasting) your energy to alter what you cannot change, is a unique human resource, and a valuable component of reframing. Acceptance isn't a sense of resignation or defeat. Rather, it is a sense of liberation that allows you to release any emotional baggage and move on with your life. Acceptance may be an overnight epiphany for some, but for most people it's an attitude that takes several days, weeks, or months to adopt.

The Power of Positive Affirmations

If you were to eavesdrop on the continuous stream of your conscious thoughts, you might be surprised to hear whispers of sabotage. The overbearing voice of the ego is constantly striving to dominate the passionate voice of the soul. By the time most people reach their late teens, the ego has practically declared victory! Sometimes the voice of the ego sounds like background static. Other times it sounds like blaring headline news. The ego best communicates throughout the landscape of the mind by providing a steady stream of negative or fear-based thoughts, attitudes, beliefs, and perceptions that, over time, begin to cloud almost everything you see.

Renowned psychologist Carl Jung referred to the constant mental chatter of the ego as "psychic tension." Many people suffer from this type of stress; however, there is a way to break this cycle and redirect your thoughts in a positive direction. Jung called this "psychic equilibrium," and the balance of this mind-set is within the grasp of each individual—including you!

Using an apt metaphor, the negative voice of the ego that feeds subliminal (and perhaps obvious) messages of fear is similar to the broadcast of a local radio station. The good news is that there is a better choice of quality programming to listen to, primarily the optimistic voice that provides a clear message about your highest qualities and your inner resources (e.g., humor, creativity, faith) to reach your highest human potential.

If you were to talk to people who have groomed themselves for success, from Olympic athletes and Grammy-winning musicians to the countless untold heroes of every age, you would find that they have learned to switch the mind's message track from the nagging voice of the ego to the passionate, grounded voice of the soul. In doing so, they have become the master of their destiny on the voyage of their highest human potential. You can do this too! People like Rosa Parks and Google creator Sergey Brin learned that confidence is not the same thing as arrogance. Positive affirmations become the mind's compass, leading the way toward humble success.

Developing Your Mastery of Reframing and Optimism

Grooming your mind's thoughts is a skill that takes practice, but it's not impossible. A quick study of elite athletes and Broadway actors reveals that they didn't get to the top by listening to the negative voice in their head. They redirected their thoughts toward an optimistic belief system. The following are steps toward making those changes:

1. The first step of reframing a situation is to gain an awareness of your thoughts and feelings. When you encounter a difficult situation, get in the habit of asking yourself how you feel, as well as why you feel this way. If you need validation of your perceptions, consider asking a friend for his or her honest opinion.

2. Once you have become familiar with the recurring pattern of your thoughts and feelings, the next step is to match each negative thought with a positive thought. In essence, find something positive in the negative situation—and there is always something positive in every bad situation. Every situation, good, bad, and ugly, offers a valuable life lesson, and when this is acknowledged, something good can be gleaned from it.

3. **Toxic thoughts** about a situation act like a mirror image to our own thoughts about ourselves, and they can have an immense negative impact on our self-esteem. Another step in the reframing process is to take an inventory of your personal strengths. By doing so, you begin to focus on your positive attributes rather than aspects that contribute to low self-esteem.

4. The last step for adopting a positive mind-set is to include the ageless wisdom of counting your blessings. Rather than focusing on what's not right, shift your attention to all that is right. Consider the concept of the self-fulfilling prophecy, which others call the law of universal attraction. It states that the more you think about negative things, the more negative things come into your life for you to think about. And the more you think about positive things, the more positive things come into your life for you to think about. In essence, to a large extent, you attract into your life that which you think about most.

Remember, negativity and the repeated thought processes that produce it can become a downward spiral of consciousness.

Tips to Incorporate the Practice of Reframing

There are many ways to shift the focus of your attention from a negative mind-set to a neutral or positive frame of mind. Remember that reframing isn't a denial of the situation; rather, it is a positive twist that acts to first recognize, and then neutralize, the sting of a potentially bad situation. Try these suggestions:

1. When you find a situation to be stressful, ask yourself what can be learned from the situation.

2. When you find yourself in a stressful circumstance, take a moment to grieve for the situation and then try to come up with between three and five things for which you are grateful.

3. When things don't go as planned (unmet expectations), rather than focusing on your negative attributes, come up with three positive aspects about yourself that you know are your personal strengths. Then pick one and start to use it. Examples include creativity, humor, and faith.

4. To cultivate a positive mind-set in nonstressful times so that you have it to use during stressful times, place a short list of positive affirmations on your bathroom mirror or computer monitor.

Exercise 4.1 invites you to try your hand at the reframing process.

Tips to Incorporate the Practice of Positive Affirmations

Effective positive affirmations have a few things in common:

- The use of "I am" to begin each statement (e.g., "I am a wonderful human being" or "I am confident of my abilities to succeed in this endeavor")
- Scripting the phrase in the affirmative (e.g., "I am going to make it" versus "I am not going to make it")
- Scripting the phrase in the present tense (e.g., "I am succeeding in this endeavor" versus "I am going to succeed in this endeavor")
- Combining the use of your affirmation with visualizing a symbolic image to combine the dynamic efforts of the conscious and unconscious minds

The following are empowering affirmations—suggestions offered for your internal self-talk—to awaken the often slumbering human spirit. The purpose is for you to consciously reprogram and incorporate these thoughts into the perpetually running chatter of your conscious and unconscious minds so that you may achieve what Jung called psychic equilibrium or mental homeostasis—the foundation for all success.

The ultimate goal in this process is to reclaim your mental and spiritual sovereignty, which in turn allows you to transition from inertia to inspiration, from victim to victor on the path of what Joseph Campbell called "the hero's journey."

Please feel free to embellish, edit, and adapt any or all of the following affirmations to best suit your needs. Keep in mind that, as with any new skill, these statements might seem awkward at first, yet after a few sessions they will begin to feel quite normal—in fact, second nature. Soon you will notice that these thoughts, these affirmations, will become integrated into your normal thinking process, particularly in times of personal challenge, and will brightly color everything you do with confidence and grace.

1. I am calm and relaxed. (Or: My body is calm and relaxed.)
2. I am grateful for all the many blessings in my life, even those that appear to be less than desirable.
3. I seek balance in my life by bringing an optimistic perspective to everyday challenges, big and small.

Exercise 4.2 asks you to think of all that is going "right" in your life.

Best Benefits of Reframing

The benefits of reframing and positive affirmations are amazing. With a new focus on life through an optimistic lens, your world will transform from black and white to full color. This is not to say that you are fooling yourself into thinking that life is a continual vacation at Disney World or that you are in denial with a Pollyanna perspective. Rather, reframing and positive affirmations become one of many resources to strengthen your resiliency during stressful times.

Chapter Summary

- Positive thinking, one form of reframing, isn't a denial of reality; rather, it is an approach to balance the ego's constant running commentary of negativity.
- The ego can generate negative thoughts, but it has been suggested that it is influenced by the media in very subtle ways to chip away at one's self-esteem.
- One aspect of reframing suggests focusing on what we have rather than what we don't have, to have an attitude of gratitude because it's hard to be stressed when you are grateful.
- Reframing invites us to look at the big picture and not see ourselves as victims. Some things we cannot change. Acceptance is a coping technique that empowers us to deal with that which we cannot change and move on with our lives.
- The power of positive affirmations suggests that unless we employ both the conscious and the unconscious minds, no amount of positive self-talk will change anything.
- To master the art of reframing and optimism, one needs to cultivate the skills of the mind.

Additional Resources

There are many great books on the topic of positive affirmations and reframing, a selection of which is listed here. There also are many wonderful guided mental imagery CDs with tracks that include positive affirmations.

Books

Brown, B. *Daring Greatly*. New York, NY: Avery Books; 2015.

Campbell, J. *The Hero with a Thousand Faces*, 3rd ed. Princeton, NJ: Princeton Bollinger; 2008.

Dyer, W. *The Power of Intention*. Carlsbad, CA: Hay House; 2005.

Frankl, V. *Man's Search for Meaning*. New York, NY: Pocket; 1974.

Frederickson, B. *Positivity*. New York, NY: Crown; 2009.

Maltz, M. *The New Psycho-Cybernetics*. New York, NY: Prentice Hall Press; 2001.

Murphy, J. *The Power of Your Subconscious Mind*, rev. ed. Eastford, CT: Martino Publishing; 2011.

National Public Radio. *Invisibilia* (Podcast). https://www.npr.org/podcasts/510307/invisibilia. Accessed December 02, 2020.

Ornstein, R., & Sobel, D. *Healthy Pleasures*. Boston, MA: De Capo Press; 1990.

Peale, N. V. *The Power of Positive Thinking*. New York, NY: Simon & Schuster; 2005.
Ryan, M. J. *Attitude of Gratitude*, 10th Anniversary Edition. Berkeley, CA: Conari Press; 2009.
Seligman, M. *Learned Optimism*. New York, NY: Vintage; 2006.

CDs

Naparstek, B. *General Wellness*. Time Warner Audiobooks; 1993.
Seaward, B. L. *Sweet Surrender*. Boulder, CO: Inspiration Unlimited; 2003.
Shamir, I. *A Thousand Things Went Right Today*. www.yourtruenature.com.

CHAPTER 5

Creative Problem Solving

KEY TERMS

Artist
Creative blocks
Creative problem solving
Creative process

Explorer
Judge
Warrior

The Ageless Wisdom of Creativity

Problem: Anyone who has seen or heard of the viral video of the plastic straw and the green sea turtle or the iconic photo of the seahorse clinging to a plastic straw knows the catastrophic problems with single-use disposable plastic items. Single-use plastic is considered one of the biggest pollution problems when it comes to overconsumption and waste. Straws may have grabbed the headlines, but coffee cups are not far behind. Concerned about this problem, Dagny Tucker had an idea that became a solution. What if people could share coffee cups like they share other items? She created an app, invested in stainless steel cups, and networked with coffeehouses, first locally and then all over the state of Colorado. Her idea helped her form her company, Vessel Works, a coffee-cup sharing network. Founded in Boulder, Colorado, Vessel Works has spread to cities in California, Oregon, and Washington State. Vessel Works offers "stainless steel options to single use disposable items, keeping plastic out of your body, ocean and the environment." This is creative problem solving 101.

Another recent chapter of creative problem solving was written in the summer of 2020 when thousands of restaurants and businesses tried to reopen between the first and second waves of the coronavirus pandemic, integrating the challenging dynamics of social distancing while trying to maintain normal business practices and income with a reduced clientele. While some businesses were forced to close permanently, others rose to the challenge, employing very creative parameters, and made it work. The restaurants that flourished quickly adapted with takeout service.

Meanwhile, many meetings and conferences moved online to the Zoom platform. From musicians to actors, people had to learn how to reinvent themselves with an online presence (and audience), and many people who enjoyed the habit of eating out regularly began a new hobby of home cooking. Where there are problems, there is opportunity. Where there is opportunity, there is the promise of creative problem solving.

Invention, innovation, imagination, incubation, adaptation, and inspiration are but a few of the many words that come to mind when one begins to articulate the revered concept known as *creativity* and the **creative process** in which the seeds of creativity take root. One cannot help but stand in awe of such creations as da Vinci's *Mona Lisa*, Beethoven's *Fifth Symphony*, or Peter Jackson's film adaptation of J. R. R. Tolkein's *The Lord of the Rings*. Less venerated, but no less important, are inventions such as the weaving loom, automobile, jet airplane, and laptop computer. It has been said that it is the creative mind of the human species that separates us from all other species.

Necessity, it is said, is the mother of invention. Although necessity is not the same thing as stress, pushed to the limits, it can elicit the stress response very quickly. It's no secret that many creative moments come under duress, to make the unworkable work and the immovable move. Stress can prove to be a force of inspiration, which, in turn, results in some rather amazing inventions and works of art. If necessity is the mother of invention, then play certainly commands a paternal role in this unique process. Many of the world's finest creations, inventions, and innovations didn't occur during stressful episodes but rather during relaxed moments of tinkering (playing) in the garage.

Surf the Internet or social media and you will quickly realize that creativity abounds for entertainment purposes, as well as countless humorous interludes. Today practically anyone can produce a song, movie, or ebook and mass market it to the world with a few keystrokes. But the skills for creative problem solving involve more than initiating a Kickstarter campaign or designing the next cool app.

By most accounts, human beings are the only species on Planet Earth that employ the dynamics of creativity. Architectural structures, songs, drawings, and mechanical devices are just some of the many things that humans, for better or worse, leave as a legacy to the rest of the world. Ironically, in a country known for its "American ingenuity," creativity is not cultivated as a human resource skill in the education system, whereas critical thinking is encouraged and highly praised. Interestingly, today American business leaders are in search of creative talent from other parts of the world. Given the rapid rate of change today in our personal lives, as well as the changes (both large and small) in the global village, it's no secret that creative problem solving will become one of the most sought-after coping skills in all levels of human endeavors. For this reason, a review of these skills is essential in the paradigm of holistic stress management.

The Creative Process Revealed

The creative process has been inspected, dissected, and analyzed in the hope of revealing the secrets to such inventions as the light bulb, the telephone, and the

Internet. Those who have cut open the proverbial goose to see how the golden egg is formed have all come to the same conclusion: Creativity is a multifaceted process combining imagination with organization, intuition with collaboration, and more recently, the right brain's functions with the left brain's skills. In his effort to understand the creative process, scholar and author Roger von Oech identifies, in a creative way, four distinct aspects that necessitate a more thorough understanding of the often illusive, yet always in demand, creative process. Von Oech describes four aspects or roles of the creative process: the explorer, the artist, the judge, and the warrior. Let's take a closer look at these components.

- *The explorer:* The first role of the creative process begins with a search for new ideas. To find ideas you have to leave the known and venture into the unknown—in other words, you have to venture off the beaten path. The **explorer** begins to look for ideas anywhere and everywhere. The farther you go off the beaten path, the more likely you will come up with one or more original ideas. In new environments, our sensory receptors are more open to new stimuli. Where do people go to explore new ideas? Examples include art museums, hardware stores, greenhouses, travel magazines, and late-night talk radio. Thomas Alva Edison was a big advocate of the exploration process: "Make a practice to keep on the lookout for novel and interesting ideas that others have used successfully. Your idea only has to be original in the adaptation to the problem you are working on." Nobel Prize Laureate Linus Pauling put it this way: "The best way to get a good idea is to get a lot of ideas." New ideas become raw materials for the next stage of the creative process. How does one sharpen his or her exploration skills? Creative experts suggest the following: Be curious, leave your own turf, break out of your routine, and don't overlook the obvious.
- *The artist:* Once the explorer returns home with lots of raw materials to use, the **artist** grabs the relay baton and continues the creative process by incubating, manipulating, adapting, parodying, and connecting ideas until one idea surfaces as the best idea. In the role of the artist, you play with ideas. In the words of Pablo Picasso, "Every act of creation is first an act of destruction." An artist sheds all inhibitions to get his or her hands dirty by turning ideas upside down. The artist asks questions like, What if … ? After a given amount of time, the artist comes to a natural conclusion that one idea may stand out above the rest, yet presents all ideas to be judged.
- *The judge:* The **judge** plays a very crucial, yet delicate, role in the creative process. One must be flexible enough to validate the artistic abilities but critical enough to make the best selection possible. As one shifts from the artist to the judge, one shifts from the right (imaginative) brain to the left (analytical) brain. The biggest hazard in the creative process is a reshuffling of these roles so that the judge begins the process. In every attempt when the mental processing begins with judgment, creativity is stifled. The role of the judge is to select the best idea of all the ideas gathered, then pass this idea to the warrior so the idea can take flight.
- *The warrior:* A good idea that has no backing will die. The role of the **warrior** is to champion the cause of the idea and make it a reality. To be a good warrior, you have to believe in yourself. Courage is a must, but so is tough skin because

not everyone is going to be as crazy about your idea as you are. The warrior must overcome fear of failure, fear of rejection, and fear of the unknown. The warrior must be brave. Should he or she realize that the idea turned out to be less than ideal, then the creativity team reconvenes either to overhaul the first idea or scrap it entirely and select a new one.

Within you reside all four members of the creativity team—explorer, artist, judge, and warrior. Exercise 5.1 highlights these roles as four aspects of your creative process by encouraging you to wear each of these hats. Exercise 5.2 entices you to shift from a left-brain analytical mind-set to a right-brain focus and get the creative juices going in preparation for your next creative endeavor.

Jonah Lehrer, author of the best-selling book *Imagine* and a contributing editor for *Wired* magazine, describes the creative process as anything but a straight line. In his examination of creativity, from various regions of the brain involved with imagination to companies such as 3M, Apple, Google, and Pixar, which foster a sense of creativity, Lehrer cites creativity as one of the most important inner resources of the 21st century, particularly with several problems (from the personal to the global) on our collective doorstep.

Creativity: Bend, Break, and Blend?

Countless people have tried to understand (deconstruct) what many perceive as the mystical, yet elusive, creative process. Anthony Brandt and David Eagleman, authors of the book, *The Runaway Species*, outlined this new take on creativity. They were stimulated by the question "How can we get different/better results from old methods, resources, and technology?" and came up with a threefold process: The creative process, they believe, has three specific cognitive strategies that create many new options when applied to problem solving. These three strategies include: (1) bending, (2) breaking, and (3) blending. *Bending* is described as reworking something that already exists while offering a new perspective and possibilities when looked at through a different mind-set (e.g., Picasso's idea of a portrait). *Breaking* goes one step further in the creative process by dismantling what worked for one technology in a limited capacity while offering more possibilities when looking at the pieces that make up the whole (e.g., smartphone towers that literally broke up the way microwaves were transported [in cells] and with greater efficiency than radio or television signals did; another example includes organ donations). The concept of *blending* combines two or more resources in a new way to achieve something that was never thought of before this alchemy of ideas (e.g., the idea of combining a woman and a fish to create a mermaid). Which of these mental strategies can you consider employing when problem solving your stressors to find a path of resolution? See Exercise 5.3.

Unlocking Your Creative Powers

Everybody is creative, but not everyone chooses to use this inherent skill. When people are stuck in fear and anxiety, 10 times out of 10—not 9 or 8 times, but 10 times out of 10—fear becomes the motivating force, immobilizing people, and inhibiting their creative skills. In the effort to understand the creative process, leaders in this field have come to understand that they must also address roadblocks that obstruct the creative process. The following, as outlined in Roger von Oech's best-selling book, *A Whack on the Side of the Head*, are a few of the more common **creative blocks** that must be dismantled before these valuable coping skills can allow us to reach our highest potential:

1. *Me? Creative?* The biggest block to the creative process is the belief that you are not creative. The roots of this belief typically sprout early in childhood when creative efforts are met by others with scorn rather than enthusiasm, which sends a message of inadequacy. Rather than looking inept, most people simply forgo their creative skills and let this muscle atrophy. The truth is that everyone is creative, but creativity, like any other skill, takes practice. If you think you are not creative, you will fulfill your limitations. Instead, learn to see yourself as the creative genius you really are. Start with small projects, such as cooking a fine meal or writing a poem. Then work your way up to bigger projects.

2. *No time for play.* Remember that play is a critical factor in the creative process. Kids love to play, but adults soon forget the freedom of play as more and more responsibilities invade their lives. Play is critical in the role of the artist, and play is always more fun when it includes others. Consider inviting some friends to join you in playtime. Playtime can include anything from a mental health day of downhill skiing to wandering the aisles of Home Depot. For play to be effective, keep ego at home when you venture out!

3. *Perfection is stifling.* Nobody likes to make a mistake, and surely not in front of an audience. Rest assured that embarrassment and humiliation are forms of fear-based stress. Ironically, the truth is that the creative process involves mistakes. In the words of Woody Allen, "If you are not failing every now and then, it's a sign that you are not trying anything very innovative." In the words of IBM founder Thomas J. Watson, "The way to success is to double your rate of failure." Edison failed with over 1,000 types of filaments for the light bulb before he found one that worked. We might still be in the dark if he gave up on number 900. Follow Edison's advice: Learn to focus on the positive, not the negative, and then keep going.

4. *But there's only one way, right?* The ego loves to be right and will do all it can to prove it is right. Ironically, in the creative process, there are many right answers. On occasion, there may be a best answer, but there are always many right answers. Looking for the right answer means stepping out of the box, exploring the unknown, and finding many answers from which to choose. In the words of French philosopher Emile Chartier, "Nothing is more dangerous than an idea when it is the only one you have." Learn to become comfortable with many right answers and many possible (viable) solutions to a problem.

5. *Fear of the unknown.* Creativity is certainly stifled in an age of specialization during which professionals are kings of minutiae and the jack-of-all-trades is nowhere in sight. Once again, in an effort not to look stupid, fear overrides thought processes by claiming either ignorance or territorial turf issues and refuses to get involved. Learn to make every area yours by embracing the wonder of all aspects of life.

Are your creative efforts blocked by the fear that whatever you do might not be good enough? Exercise 5.4 is an exercise to break through these blocks by delving into the creative process and coming out a victor.

There is no denying that Apple co-founder Steve Jobs was a creative genius. His biographer, Walter Isaacson, described Steve Jobs this way: "Some leaders push innovations by being good at the big picture. Others do so by mastering details. Jobs did both, relentlessly." In the words of Steve Jobs, "'You always have to keep pushing [outside the box] to be innovative." In his now famous Think Different commercial, the narrative ends with these words: "The people who are crazy enough to think they can change the world are the ones who do. Think Different."

Boredom: An Essential Component to Creativity!

What does boredom have to do with the creative process? Apparently plenty. To really exercise the creative muscle, the mind needs downtime to incubate ideas. This doesn't happen when the mind is preoccupied and heavily engaged with social media posts, binge TV watching, or video gaming. The mind needs quiet time to engage all aspects of the creative process, yet today people are so consumed with their screen devices that the creative process is stifled. Creativity experts now agree that boredom (little or no mental activity) is essential to the creative process. As such, these same experts suggest unplugging from one's screen device and giving the mind a chance to do nothing for scheduled periods of incubating ideas. Learning to quiet the mind is considered an essential precursor in allowing the creative process to unfold.

From Creativity to Creative Problem Solving

The creative process is not a linear process with a direct route from problem to solution. If it were that easy, everyone would claim to be creative! Although the creative process isn't hard, it's not direct either. To use von Oech's metaphor of the four roles of creativity, most likely you will be switching hats often, from explorer to warrior, until it becomes obvious the problem is solved with complete satisfaction (**Figure 5.1**). The following is a tried-and-true method of **creative problem solving**. Once you have read through this process, Exercise 5.5 provides this same template to be used for any current problems you are facing that demand a creative solution.

1. *Describing the problem:* Take time to identify and describe the problem. Sometimes the answer can be found in how the problem is identified. Consider being playful in this first step, such as describing the problem as a child might see it or as an alien might view it. Using the method of dividing and conquering, try breaking down the problem into smaller pieces.
2. *Generating ideas:* What to cook for dinner tonight? Come up with five selections. Where to take your next vacation? Come up with five possible ideas. How to pay for your college education? Come up with five viable solutions. Generating ideas is the fun stage of the creative problem-solving process. To do

a good job generating ideas, learn to get comfortable stepping out of your comfort zone (the box) and venture out to search for great ideas.

3. *Selecting and refining the idea:* Once you have several ideas, you can begin to narrow down the selection to the best idea. To pick the best idea, consider playing the game What If. Try to imagine the idea already implemented and see how it works. Visualize it. Think the idea through to its desired result. Ask yourself what the pros and cons are. Although you won't know till you try, selection involves both intuition and imagination as well as good judgment skills.

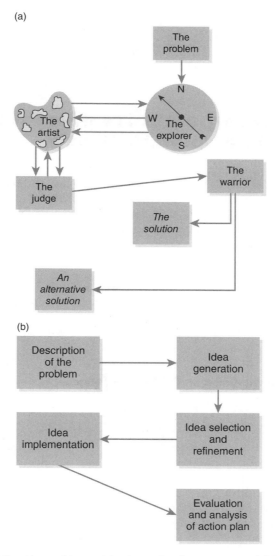

Figure 5.1 (a) Creative problem solving is rarely a linear process. (b) The map of creative problem solving.

4. *Implementing the idea:* Putting an idea into play can take minutes or weeks, depending on the problem begging to be solved. The implementation of every idea requires some risk as well as some faith that it will work. Implementation means taking the first step back into the unknown. It may mean making a phone call or getting in your car and driving somewhere. It may mean sitting down and talking with someone, and most likely it will mean participating in a collaborative effort to pull it off. Fear inhibits this stage of the creative process, but don't let it! Remember: Face your fear and it will disappear!

5. *Evaluating and analyzing the idea:* When ideas work, and in this case when the crisis is over, people tend to forget the magic that made it happen. But success begs to be highlighted by taking a good look so that the lessons can be learned should they be needed again. It's a good habit to study successes as well as unmet expectations; valuable lessons can be learned from both ends of the creative process.

How to Incorporate Creative Problem Solving into Your Life Routine

The best way to incorporate creative problem-solving skills into your life routine is to follow the template in Exercise 5.5 for any and all problems. Reading books on creativity can help (and is strongly encouraged) you develop creative problem-solving skills, but reading about doing something and actually doing it are two different things. Be on the lookout for how others solve their problems. Adaptation of ideas to your unique situation can prove to be very empowering!

The next best way to enhance your creative skills is to practice them, even in areas that are totally unrelated to problems begging for resolution. There is a wonderful transfer effect from the creative process with music, photography, cooking, or writing about the problems and dilemmas that face us each day. Engaging in small acts of creativity gives one the courage to try bigger things. When looking to initiate the creative problem-solving process, start small (e.g., What should I prepare for dinner tonight?).

Best Benefits of Creative Problem Solving

Everyone holds the keys to creativity; however, there are those who refuse to believe they are holding the keys in their hands. There are two kinds of people in this world: Those who think they are creative and those who don't. The people who believe they are creative are, indeed, very creative. Perhaps as no surprise, the people who don't believe they are creative are not creative. Creativity is a very empowering inner resource. Tackling a problem through ingenuity makes you feel like you can conquer the world. By engaging fully in the creative process, you learn to let go of fears and anxieties that tend to hold you back, allowing you to sail ahead on the river of life.

Chapter Summary

- The creative process is very empowering as an effective coping technique for stressors, both big and small.
- The creative process is known to have four aspects; the first two (the explorer and the artist) are considered right brain, whereas the second two (the judge and the warrior) are considered left brain. The combined process is a whole brain activity.
- Ego-generated thoughts of fear combine to be the biggest impediment to the creative process. Unlocking your creative powers first involves deactivating the ego.
- Creative problem solving takes the creative process and applies it to resolving stressful issues. There are five steps, from identifying the process to evaluating the solution.
- Incorporating the skills of creative problem solving begins with knowing the aspects of the creative process and then applying them to each problem that begs for resolution.
- Benefits of creative problem solving include empowerment and promoting high self-esteem.

Additional Resources

Brandt, A., & Eagleman, D. *The Runaway Species*. New York, NY: Catapult; 2017.

Gelb, M. *How to Think Like Leonardo da Vinci*. New York, NY: Dell/Random House; 2000.

Isaacson, W, *Steve Jobs*. New York, NY: Simon & Schuster; 2013.

Lehrer, J. *Imagine: How Creativity Works*. Boston, MA: Houghton Mifflin Harcourt; 2012.

McMeekin, G. *The 12 Secrets of Highly Creative Women*. Berkeley, CA: Conari Press; 2011.

Michalko, M. *Cracking Creativity*. Berkeley, CA: Ten Speed Press; 2011.

Thorp, T. *The Creative Habit*. New York, NY: Simon & Schuster; 2003.

TIME. *The Science of Creativity*. August 3, 2018. Time Magazine, Special Edition.

von Oech, R. *Creative Whack Pack*. New York, NY: Warner; 1992.

von Oech, R. *A Kick in the Seat of the Pants*. New York, NY: Perennial; 1986.

Stress Relief Techniques

CHAPTER 6

Nutrition: Eating for a Healthy Immune System

KEY TERMS

Bioflavonoids
Essential fatty acids
Excitotoxins

Genetically modified organisms (GMOs)
Organic food

The Ageless Wisdom of Healthy Eating

If there is one thing the COVID pandemic taught us, it is that we should never take eating out at restaurants, as well as food purchasing and food preparation, for granted. Moreover, the term *comfort food* took on a whole new meaning in 2020, as people began to examine and reexamine personal eating habits, cooking habits, and our relationship to food. A new term emerged during the pandemic: *food fatigue*, describing the boredom of eating the same meals day after day. In turn, the importance of high-quality, nutrient-dense food has become even more important in regard to the health of our immune systems.

Since the beginning of time, food has played an essential, if not critical, role in the survival of the human species. Over the ages, food was hunted, gathered, and grown, not only for nutrients and energy but also for health and the restoration of health from disease and illness. Plants in the form of fruits, vegetables, legumes, and herbs were critical to one's diet. In addition, food (specifically, "comfort foods") is a great pacifier, and there is no denying that certain foods can exalt the senses to a state of euphoria in a way that no other means can. Combined with great company, eating is known as one of the greatest means of happiness.

For all these reasons, it's not an understatement to say that nutrition used to be taken very seriously because life depended on it. In essence, eating food was considered to be the first course of action to take to maintain health and well-being. Ironically, today much of the food available is the cause of many diseases and illnesses, rather than a means to prevent a decline in one's health. At no time in the history of the United States have food choices been so great, yet the quality of food so questionable. For millennia, nutrition was first and foremost a health issue; however, today health concerns are grossly outweighed by economic and political concerns. One only needs to be reminded how cows (known herbivores) became mad in the first place. They were fed rendered parts of other cows, lambs, and chicken feces, all mixed in with their grain cereal.

During the past few decades, a large, uncontrolled experiment has been conducted on the American population through the introduction of synthetic sub- stances into food production. With the introduction of synthetic hormones, antibiotics, pesticides, herbicides, fungicides, fertilizers, artificial sweeteners, artifi- cial fats, food brighteners, and most recently genetically modified foods, Americans have seen a corresponding rise in a variety of chronic diseases. Some foods contain so many chemicals that there is literally no place for them on the U.S. government's MyPlate recommendations, yet people consume vast quantities of them every day. A case in point occurred in 2001 when Kellogg's Corn Flakes and Taco John taco shells were recalled due to the amount of pesticides found in them. The year 2004 saw the first case of mad cow disease in the United States, something Americans were assured would never happen.

Several years ago, the American Cancer Society (ACS) stated that although the death rate due to cancer had decreased due to early detection, one out of every three people would contract cancer in their lifetime. They also stated that 60 percent of all cancer could be eliminated if people would choose a healthier diet. Apparently, people's appeals for good taste have won out over their concern for health in the 24/7, fast-paced American lifestyle. The ACS might as well have been shouting in the wind, because its warning seems to have gone unheeded.

In an effort to promote shelf life and increase profits, the major food corpora- tions concoct ingenious ways to keep food looking and tasting fresh. We now know that chemical preservatives, hydrogenated fats, and scores of other synthetic com- ponents used in the process of food production certainly prolong shelf life, but they appear to do absolutely nothing to promote health. Instead, they compromise it. Today synthetic food is a stressor to the body, specifically the immune system. With all we know about the microbiome (and all we have to learn), given that 70 percent of the immune system is contained in the GI tract, what you eat has a direct effect on the integrity of your immune system. For this reason, we should all be more mindful of what we eat.

Even if there weren't such an influx of synthetic foods, there are a series of problems that occur regarding nutrition and stress. Each problem itself is easy to rectify; however, as these problems mount, their combined effects pose a greater danger to the integrity of your health. Metaphorically speaking, there are four dom- inos that tumble in a progression of a stressed lifestyle, the result of which signifi- cantly compromises one's physiology:

- *Stress domino #1:* Under the physiological demands of the stress response, the body's requirement for energy increases, regardless of whether the actions of fight or flight are used. In simple terms, more glucose is released into the bloodstream as a source of immediate energy. Then, more free fatty acids are released, just in case they are needed for long-term energy. The net result of these and other metabolic reactions to the stress response is a depletion of both macronutrients (carbohydrates, fats, proteins) and micronutrients (vitamins, minerals). As the micronutrients are depleted, the efficiency of their metabolic response becomes compromised until they are replaced.

- *Stress domino #2:* Sadly, as a rule, when people are stressed, good eating habits are the first thing to go, particularly in a hectic schedule. Home-cooked meals are replaced with convenient fast foods. As was noted in the book *Fast Food Nation*, fast foods are processed for taste, not nutrition. The vast majority of these foods contain what are known in nutrition circles as "empty calories," meaning they have little or no nutritional value. The consequence of bad eating habits is that the nutrients depleted during prolonged periods of stress are not replaced. Hence, the body's physiological systems operate less efficiently. Many systems are compromised, including the immune system and the reproductive system. Under compromised conditions, the body tries to compensate, but over time even these backup systems fail. The end result is a host of physiological problems that lead to poor health.

- *Stress domino #3:* As if it's not bad enough that valuable nutrients are depleted during prolonged stress, and many of these nutrients are not replaced, many fast foods, junk foods, and convenience foods contain substances that act on the nervous system to keep the stress response elevated, including these:

  - *Caffeine:* Coffee, tea, soda pop, and chocolate contain a constituent found in caffeine called methylated xanthine, a substance known to trigger the release of epinephrine and norepinephrine, which in turn increase heart rate, blood pressure, and other metabolic activities in the preparation for fight or flight.

  - *Refined sugar:* Research suggests that refined or bleached sugar can have an effect on the nervous system similar to what caffeine has. It's no secret that processed foods are high in refined sugar. High fructose corn syrup and table sugar are two examples of refined sugar.

  - *Refined flour:* As with refined sugar, refined flour appears to affect the nervous system and, in some cases, the adrenal (stress) glands.

  - *Salt (sodium):* Salt is known to cause the body to retain water. Water retention tends to increase blood pressure. Although only one teaspoon of salt is recommended per day, processed food is loaded with salt to appease the taste buds.

- *Stress domino #4:* A new term has entered the American lexicon regarding the proliferation of toxic chemical residues found in the body: *bio-burden.* It describes the amounts of toxic chemical substances that are found in the body's blood and tissue samples, including mother's milk. Not only do processed foods contain a plethora of chemicals, but the skin also absorbs chemicals from makeup, shampoos, hair dyes, deodorants, sunblock, and other substances applied topically to the skin. The effects of these substances on humans are not conclusive, but in animal studies the results are disturbing. Suffice to say that even in trace amounts these chemical residues become a stressor to the body's physiology and immune system, challenging the integrity of one's overall health and well-being. Please turn to Exercise 6.1 and evaluate your stress-related eating behaviors.

Food Allergies and GMOs

On Saturday, May 22, 2013, millions of people around the world gathered in a unified demonstration to protest the American company Monsanto, notorious for its efforts to genetically modify food (e.g., splicing the herbicide Roundup in corn). Protests have continued in cities across the world ever since. Cross-species tinkering with DNA is not without its consequences. With the rise in GMO (genetically modified organism) foods (ranging from the herbicide Roundup in corn to the genes of flounder in tomatoes to prevent frostbite), so too has there been a rise in food allergies. The proverbial question becomes this: When you place a gene of a flounder into a tomato plant, is it an animal or a vegetable? Less than a week after global protests, scientists were quite surprised to find genetically modified wheat in a field in Oregon. Although genetically modified corn and soy are permitted by the U.S. government, genetically modified wheat is not! Wheat, high in protein, creates bigger yields for farmers and is considered more drought resistant. It also is considered harder to digest and absorb. It is estimated that over 30 percent of Americans are now gluten intolerant (gluten is the protein source in wheat, rye, and barley). The Mayo Clinic estimates that 1 in 110 people have celiac disease (dire wheat intolerance). Wheat products range from bread and hamburger buns to breadcrumbs, cereals, soups, imitation crab, mashed potatoes, some spices, and many sauces. Well beyond eggs, peanuts, and milk, people today suffer from a great many food allergies. GMO foods may be to blame, as these genetic "creations" are considered by some to be a foreign pathogen (a stressor) to the human immune system. It is estimated that over 65 percent of foods sold in grocery stores are genetically modified, all unlabeled as a result of powerful corporate lobbying efforts.

About Water

Although it contains no calories, water is often acknowledged as being the most important nutrient. In simple terms, we would die quickly (in a matter of days) without it. Although the average person does drink a fair amount of beverages, most people do not consume enough water. Instead coffee, teas, and soft drinks act as diuretics, resulting in a moderate state of dehydration. As the rule goes, if you are thirsty, most likely you are already showing signs of dehydration.

Signs of dehydration include sluggishness, fatigue, headaches, low energy, and poor appetite. This not only stresses the body's physiology but also may increase emotional stress regarding other life issues. Many proponents of rehydration suggest drinking eight glasses of water per day, but the real test to see if you are drinking enough water is to check the color of your urine. Nearly clear urine is the goal. One good goal is to drink a glass of water soon after you awake because the body has gone roughly 8 hours without any fluids.

Best Benefits of Healthy Eating

The benefits of healthy eating are too numerous to mention, but suffice to say that sound nutritional practices play a crucial role in nearly every aspect of health, from eyesight to kidney function. Moreover, poor nutritional habits only add to the critical mass of stress that people face each day. The human body has an amazing ability to adapt to the stress placed on it. For this reason, poor eating habits tend to result in chronic illnesses rather than acute problems. The good news is that the body, by and large, has the great gift of resiliency, meaning that by making healthy changes in your diet, your body has a better chance to begin and sustain the healing process. Today, healthy eating requires some vigilance with regard to the food industry; however, at the same time, you could drive yourself nuts trying to avoid all the potholes in the national food chain. For this reason, it's best to be cautious, but not neurotic, about your food choices.

How to Incorporate the Practice of Healthy Eating into Your Life Routine

Hippocrates, the father of modern medicine, once said, "Let food be your medicine and let medicine be your food." Unfortunately today, rather than consuming food as medicine, the vast majority of people consume it as poison. Like toxins dumped into a river, the human body can take only so much before signs of disease and illness manifest. The following is a list of suggestions to tip the scale back to balance and promote a sense of health and well-being:

1. *Consume a good supply of antioxidants.* Antioxidants fight the damage of free radicals that destroy cell membranes, DNA, RNA, and mitochondria. Antioxidants can be found in foods containing beta-carotene, vitamin C, vitamin E, and the mineral selenium. If you were to take a look at the eating habits of indigenous tribes around the world, you would notice that the greatest amount of calories in their diet comes from vegetables. Vegetables contain not only a rich supply of vitamins, minerals, and fiber but also a wonderful supply of antioxidants, nature's antidote to free radicals. Research in the field of nutrition has begun to reveal that antioxidants can be found in a variety of natural food sources, including vegetables, fruits, and herbs.

2. *Consume a good supply of fiber (30–40 grams/day with organic vegetables).* Fiber helps clean the colon of toxic materials that might otherwise be absorbed into the bloodstream. The average American eats about 5–8 grams of fiber daily, far below the recommended amount. There is not a lot of fiber in iceberg lettuce, but there is plenty to be found in dark-green leafy veggies, citrus fruits, and legumes. Fiber also helps regulate the elimination process of your bowels. Under the best conditions, typical transit time from mouth to rectum is about 12–18 hours. Experts suggest that there should be one bowel movement per meal. For the average person who eats three meals a day, this would mean three bowel movements; however, many people confide to their physicians that their average is more like one per day. Waste that doesn't get removed becomes toxic to the colon and affects the whole body. Colon cancer is the third most prevalent type of cancer in the United States.

3. *Drink plenty of fresh, clean (filtered) water.* As mentioned, water acts as a transport system to remove toxic waste produced by each cell to the kidneys, where it can be excreted. Dehydration tends to compromise the body's ability to remove toxic waste. Toxins that are not flushed out cause damage of all kinds at the cellular level.

An article in *National Geographic* stated that only 1 percent of the world's water is drinkable. News reports suggest that fresh water will become the issue of the decade. (The United Nations has even suggested that wars will be fought over water.) Toxicologists have noted that agricultural runoff from industrial farms into our national waterways has infiltrated our water supply. Moreover, water specialists have noted an increase in pharmaceutical by-products (e.g., Zoloft, Prozac, birth control pills) in our drinking water, which may be related to a score of health problems. As you can see, water safety is already an issue. In addition, water filtration plants use huge amounts of chlorine and fluoride in their water treatment procedures, all of which end up in our tap water. For this reason, it is a great idea to install your own water filtration system as a means to purify the water you drink. Bottled water may sound like a good idea, but supplies of bottled water are stored in warehouses for prolonged periods of time, allowing the chemicals from plastic residue to seep into the water. Water stored in BPA-free hard (non-bendable) plastic is the only recommended water product, suggesting you may wish to bring your own bottled water with you. A good goal to determine if you are drinking enough water is the excretion of nearly clear urine.

4. *Decrease consumption of foods treated with pesticides, fungicides, and herbicides.* These substances are toxic and many are carcinogenic. Eat **organic food** whenever possible. Current research reveals that we consume large amounts of synthetic estrogens from the foods we eat. Synthetic estrogens are used in a host of agricultural products, such as fertilizers, pesticides, fungicides, and herbicides. (They are also found in animal food products when these substances are used in the animals' feed.) These toxins are found on the exterior of fruits and veggies to be washed off, but they are also taken up by the root system and deposited in the stems, leaves, and fruits of these plants. Once toxins are consumed, it's the role of the liver to filter them out, but the liver can do only so much, and those chemicals that slip back into the bloodstream are transported to fatty tissue. Long before the word *organic* was introduced to the American lexicon, the word *natural* conveyed a sense of the pristine nature of foods that were undisturbed by the agricultural complex. Today, the word *natural* has become a marketing term and rarely does it mean what the word originally described. Today, the difference between natural and organic is this: Unlike foods described as natural, 100 percent organic connotes that the soil in which the plants are grown has been clean of synthetic chemicals and pesticides for a period of at least 3 years and that the crops grown on the soil have been exposed to only natural fertilizers (such as seaweeds). In 2001, Congress passed legislation requiring that certified organic food be labeled as such. Be sure to read your food labels.

5. *Consume an adequate amount of complete proteins.* White blood cells are composed of amino acids from protein sources. To ensure the intake of all essential amino acids, it is necessary to consume complete proteins. The eight amino acids that the body cannot produce must be obtained from outside food sources. Foods such as meat, fish, poultry, and eggs contain all the essential amino acids (hence the term *complete*), whereas many grains and legumes do not. If you are not a vegetarian, this really isn't a concern; but if you are, it is important to know how to complement your protein sources to ensure you are getting all the essential amino acids. Because amino acids are used for the production of enzymes, hormones, and the entire family of white blood cells, it is

imperative to consume adequate amounts of protein in your diet. Again, 100 percent organic is the preferred source.

6. *Decrease consumption of all processed foods (e.g., junk food, fast food)*. Here are two little-known facts: Not only does most food travel a distance of at least 1,500 miles from farm to store, but the average amount of time that packaged food remains on the grocery store shelf is about 3–6 days, depending on your locale. If you were to check the expiration date on these packages, however, you would find that the suggested shelf life is projected in years. What allows these products to endure this long? If you read the labels, you would find a long list of preservatives composed mainly of chemicals. Once again, the role of the liver is to filter these out of the system, but the liver can do only so much. Most people's livers are overtaxed. Many of these chemicals enter the bloodstream and wreak havoc on the body. Once in the bloodstream, it becomes the job of the immune system to destroy or remove them, but an overtaxed immune system can do only so much as well. For this reason, it is best to minimize or avoid processed foods altogether. As the expression goes, "Think outside the box," particularly with processed foods, to avoid overconsumption of additives and preservatives that your body really doesn't need.

7. *Decrease/avoid the consumption of antibiotics and hormones*. Perhaps it's no coincidence that the rise in cancer corresponds to the rise of many unnatural chemicals found today in our foods. One topic of concern is the proliferation of pharmacological drugs found today in our protein sources. To stop the spread of disease among cattle, chicken, turkey, and even fish farmed in hatcheries, these animals are given massive amounts of hormones and antibiotics. Although some of these chemicals pass through, many of them are stored in the animals' muscle tissue, which is then eaten by unsuspecting consumers, whether it's bought in the grocery store or served in a restaurant. Antibiotics can have an adverse effect on the intestinal flora in your GI tract (killing the much-needed and friendly acidophilus bacteria). A significant decrease in acidophilus lays the groundwork for the yeast infection called *Candida*. *Candida*, it should be noted, is suggested by some to be the underlying cause of fibromyalgia and chronic fatigue syndrome.

8. *Consume a good supply and balance of omega-3s (e.g., from cold-water fish and flaxseed oil) and omega-6s (e.g., from vegetable oils)*. There are two **essential fatty acids** that the body cannot produce, so they must be obtained from outside sources. Ironically, there is no mention of these two essential fatty acids in the current U.S. government MyPlate dietary guidelines. Although the merits of omega-3 oils have been known for decades, surprisingly few people are aware that omega-3 is used in the synthesis of prostaglandins, whose primary role is as an anti-inflammatory agent. Long ago, cold-water fish was considered brain food. What was once considered an old wives' tale now turns out to be quite true, because omega-3s are considered an essential aspect of brain tissue (which is composed mostly of fatty tissue). The American diet is heavy in omega-6s and virtually nonexistent in omega-3s. The suggested balance between these two is a ratio of 2:1 (omega-6:omega-3).

9. *Decrease intake of saturated fats (meat and dairy products)*. Current research suggests that a diet high in saturated fat is associated with higher levels of cholesterol. But here is another interesting fact: When fats are digested and transported to the liver, they cannot travel via the bloodstream until they get to the

liver. Instead, they have to be transported via the lymphatic system. In his book *Spontaneous Healing*, Andrew Weil states that a diet high in fats tends to preoccupy the immune system with energy devoted to this delivery, thus decreasing the efficiency of the immune system. Balance is the key.

10. *Decrease/avoid intake of trans-fatty acids (partially hydrogenated oils)*. Fats that are liquid at room temperature are called lipids. Lipids are prone to becoming rancid when they are subjected to heat and light. Researchers figured out a way to decrease rancidity by changing the molecular structure of lipids to make them solid at room temperature. The process is known as hydrogenation, and today these fats are known as partially hydrogenated oils or trans-fatty acids. Trans-fatty acids are anything but natural. The current joke about trans-fatty acids is that the reason that they prolong shelf life is that bacteria won't go near them. We should be as smart. Trans-fatty acids tend to destroy cell membranes by blocking the gates that allow nutrients to go in and waste products to leave. When cells become toxic, cancer is not far behind. Trans-fatty acids, found in most baked goods, such as cereal, cookies, and tortilla shells, are associated with both coronary heart disease and cancer, and perhaps scores of other diseases we don't know about yet. These act like free radicals and should be avidly avoided.

11. *Eat a variety of food colors (fruits and vegetables with bioflavonoids)*. The Eastern traditions suggest eating foods (fruits and veggies) with a wide variety of colors. Not only does food provide energy, but the colors also provide energy to the body's core energy centers (chakras). Known as the "rainbow diet," food colors are thought to play an important role in the vitality and health of the organs associated with each chakra region: cranberry juice for urinary tract infection, tomatoes for prostate health, bilberries for the eyes, and so on. In the mid- to late 1990s, food researchers discovered that **bioflavonoids**, nonnutrients associated with food color, contain an active ingredient to help prevent cancer. The real message here is to eat a good variety of fruits and vegetables (organic whenever possible). Consider Exercise 6.2 as an invitation to evaluate your food color intake.

12. *Consume a good balance of foods with proper pH*. The body's acid/alkaline balance is very delicate. Although it is assumed that by the time food particles have been digested for absorption, they do not disturb this balance, this assumption is now questioned because recent discoveries suggest that cancerous tumors are more likely to grow in an acidic environment. Many processed and pasteurized foods are acidic, thus tipping the scales toward a body more prone to cancer. Proponents of raw foods (fruits and veggies) suggest that this type of diet helps the body regain its balance toward the magic number 7 on the acid/alkaline scale. This might be something to consider for those people who have cancer.

13. *Replenish nutrients consumed by the stress response*. The stress response (fight or flight) demands energy, in the form of both carbohydrates (glucose) and fats (lipids). If you are experiencing chronic stress, more than likely you are using and possibly depleting a host of essential nutrients. A whole series of metabolic reactions that require vitamins and minerals is necessary to have these nutrients available for use. The following are believed to be involved with energy metabolism and thus must be replaced on a regular basis under stress: B complex vitamins (B6, B12), vitamin C, magnesium, calcium, chromium, copper, iron, and zinc.

14. *Decrease consumption of simple sugars*. It is believed that the average person consumes two to three times his or her body weight in refined sugar each year.

Perhaps it's human nature to have a sweet tooth but, as the saying goes, everything in moderation. A diet high in refined sugar sets the stage for many health problems. Aside from overtaxing the pancreas to regulate blood sugar levels with the release of insulin, it is suggested that cancer cells thrive on a high simple-sugar diet. Some reports suggest that refined sugar also decreases white blood cell count. All of this implies that a diet high in refined sugar is a threat to your immune system.

15. *Decrease/avoid "excitotoxins."* As noted in the critically acclaimed book **Excitotoxins**, aspartame (Nutrasweet) and monosodium glutamate (MSG) inhibit brain function by crossing the blood–brain barrier, thus affecting cognitive functions, including response time, decision making, attention span, and memory. Pilots for several national airlines are forbidden to drink any beverage or food (even gum) with aspartame. Current research reveals that when not refrigerated, the two amino acids that combine to form this artificial sweetener go through a chemical reaction resulting in the formation of formaldehyde. In laboratory studies, formaldehyde is shown to compromise the integrity of the immune system. MSG is also cited as an excitotoxin. Due to agreements made with the U.S. Food and Drug Administration (FDA), MSG is not listed on food labels as monosodium glutamate; rather, it is simply listed as "spice." Read the labels and avoid excitotoxins!

16. *Moderate your consumption of alcohol.* A high intake of alcohol (more than two glasses a day) is said to compromise liver and immune function. Current studies reveal that excessive alcohol consumption decreases the efficiency of the immune system, thus making one more vulnerable to the effects of bacteria, viruses, and other pathogens that make their way into the body. Although studies show that red wine can increase levels of high-density lipoproteins (HDLs, the good cholesterol) in the blood, moderation is the key to good health.

17. *Prepare food in the best way possible.* Even though you may think you are getting an adequate amount of vitamins and minerals, you may be losing these nutrients, depending on how you cook your foods. Many vitamins are destroyed with high amounts of heat, which is why microwave ovens are not recommended. Veggies should be steamed, not cooked in water, because water-soluble vitamins and minerals are leached out during boiling and lost when they are poured down the drain with the excess water. A new health food trend these days is the raw food diet, which advocates eating vegetables and fruits uncooked so that the full array of vitamins, minerals, and enzymes is available to the human body for absorption.

18. *Eat organic and free-range meats whenever possible.* Due to the increasing presence of hormones and antibiotics in beef, chicken, and other animal products, it is highly recommended to eat organic and free-range animal products. The term *free range* was introduced to convey a sense that animals were free to roam and eat natural vegetation. Check with your butcher, because this is not always the case. With the introduction of mad cow disease and chronic wasting disease in recent years, eating organic has taken on a whole new importance. Buffalo is a good meat choice, because to date this is one animal that hasn't been tinkered with.

19. *Avoid* **genetically modified organisms** (GMOs, *also known as Frankenfoods), which are known to promote allergy problems.* For centuries, farmers have experimented with plants through grafts and cross-fertilization to come up with new variations of plant species, from fruits (seedless oranges) to flowers

(the variegated tulip). It wasn't until the late 1990s that scientists began to pull genes from one species (e.g., flounder) and place them in the DNA of another (e.g., tomato), hence playing God with our food supply. We now have super tomatoes that can withstand a cold frost. The problem arises when, because of genetic engineering, people with an allergy to one food (nuts) find themselves having an acute allergic reaction to food they previously were able to eat (corn). A dramatic rise in food allergies has been linked to a corresponding influx of genetically modified foods. Current estimates suggest that over half of the food bought in local grocery stores is genetically modified, yet due to political pressure by food corporations, you will never see this on a food label. GMOs are a burden to the immune system, which doesn't recognize this unnatural concoction. Allergic reactions are a message from your immune system that something is terribly amiss. Again, organic foods are your safest bet.

20. *Use herbal therapies to boost your immune system.* Long before the Bayer company patented aspirin, herbs were (and in many countries still are) the primary source of healing to bring the body back to a sense of homeostasis. Today, pharmaceutical companies are spending millions to replicate the active ingredients of various herbs, yet traditional herbalists will tell you that the best results occur by going directly to the plant itself. If that's not possible, consider tinctures or teas. Herbs and spices that are known to help boost or activate the immune system include astragalus; shiitake, maitake, and reishi mushrooms; turmeric; osha; and echinacea. Milk thistle is also good for helping the liver cleanse toxins from the body, and in this day and age, everyone could use milk thistle. Linda Whitedove is a traditional herbalist practicing in Boulder, Colorado, and a former consultant for Home Grown Herbals. She is the first herbalist hired by her local hospital in the department of integrative medicine to work alongside physicians. As a guest speaker in my nutrition course, Linda had this to say about the connection between herbs and chronic illness: "Not long ago, people used many herbs and spices when preparing foods, such as rosemary, oregano, thyme, coriander, cilantro, and basil. It was the essential oils in these plants that contain many healing properties. Today most people eat out, or eat processed foods. The only natural additive they're getting is sodium and that's not even a spice. My recommendation is to cook more of your own meals and reintroduce the use of more fresh spices."

Best Benefits of Sound Nutritional Habits

After reading this chapter, you may wonder if any food is safe to eat. The answer is yes! In today's market, organic foods offer the best source of healthy nutrients for the body. Remember, the body is resilient and desires a state of wholeness. Given the chance, it will do all it can to return to a state of wholeness. This means that you can still enjoy an ice cream cone every now and then. If, however, you or a loved one is diagnosed with a chronic disease, you may wish to pull in the reins and guide your eating habits with several of these suggestions. Here is a final tip to help keep your body in balance: Consider eating at least one meal a day for your immune system.

Chapter Summary

- This chapter highlights a metaphor of stress dominos: (1) stress depletes nutrients, (2) poor eating habits don't replace needed nutrients, (3) some foods actually trigger the stress response, and (4) many foods negatively impact the immune system.
- Water is an essential nutrient, and many people don't get enough of it.
- Stress can compromise the immune system, as can many foods. However, many foods and specific eating habits can enhance the immune system.
- Consider eating at least one meal a day for your immune system.

Additional Resources

Blaylock, E. *Excitotoxins: The Taste That Kills*. Santa Fe, NM: Health Press; 1997.

Greger, M., & Stone, M. *How Not to Die*. New York, NY: Flatiron Books; 2015.

Hicks, J. M. *Healthy Eating, Healthy World*. Dallas, TX: BenBella; 2011.

Kessler, D. *The End of Overeating*. New York, NY: Rodale; 2010.

Lyman, H. *The Mad Cowboy*. New York, NY: Scribner; 2001.

Margel, D. *The Nutrient Dense Eating Plan*. Laguna Beach, CA: Basic Health; 2005.

Nestle, M. *What to Eat*. New York, NY: North Point Press; 2007.

Ornish, D. *The Spectrum*. New York, NY: Ballantine; 2008.

Pollan, M. *In Defense of Food*. New York, NY: Penguin; 2009.

Pulde, M. *The Forks Over Knives Plan*. New York, NY: Atria Books; 2017.

Roberts, P. *The End of Food*. New York, NY: Mariner; 2009.

Robins, J. *The Food Revolution*. Berkeley, CA: Conari Press; 2010.

Rountree, R., & Colman, C. *Immunotics*. New York, NY: Putnam; 2001.

Schlosser, E. *Fast Food Nation*. New York, NY: Houghton Mifflin Harcourt; 2012.

Somer, E. *Food and Mood*. New York, NY: Henry Holt; 1999.

Teitel, M., & Wilson, K. *Genetically Engineered Food*. Rochester, VT: Park Street Press; 2001.

Weil, A. *Eating Well for Optimal Health*. New York, NY: Knopf; 2001.

Weil, A. *Spontaneous Healing*. New York, NY: Knopf; 2000.

CHAPTER 7

Physical Exercise

KEY TERMS

All-or-none conditioning principle
Circadian rhythm

Energy balance
Physical exercise

The Ageless Wisdom of Physical Exercise

We begin this chapter with a news alert: The health of Americans is in serious decline. We are eating more and exercising less. We are so fixated on smartphones and computer screens throughout each waking hour of each day that we don't get outside. If we do, it's only where there is WiFi access. Humans have created an information-based society to which their bodies cannot adapt. As a consequence, many Americans (and all those planetary citizens to whom we have exported this lifestyle) are in grave danger of being overweight or obese and contracting a serious chronic disease, creating a lifetime of discomfort combined with emotional and financial hardship. Fact: Human beings were not designed to sit in front of computers or television screens, yet this describes the majority of U.S. citizens today. Sitting around all day under the cloud of the coronavirus pandemic and eating comfort foods did not go unnoticed on bathroom scales. Another new term entered the pandemic lexicon: *quarantine 15* (as in 15 pounds of additional body weight). However, if there is one upshot of the pandemic, it's that people who were experienced lockdown and social isolation month after month decided to get outdoors between the first, second, and third waves of the pandemic. Bicycle shops could not maintain inventory due to the demand for mountain bikes, trail bikes, and cruisers. The sale of park passes and fishing licenses increased dramatically. Kids were even observed playing basketball in their driveways. Will these trends continue? Time will tell.

The field of exercise physiology is relatively new as an academic discipline when compared to the fields of mathematics and physics, yet the information garnered over seven decades of research has proven to be invaluable with regard to physical health and longevity. The bottom line is that **physical exercise** is essential for health and well-being.

In the early 1970s, coronary heart disease (CHD) made headline news as the nation's number-one killer. Sadly, more than four decades later, CHD is still ranked as the number-one killer in the United States. At times, it appears that Americans have grown numb to the statistics. Today, exercise formulas can be found on cereal boxes and in infomercials, yet despite the best efforts by healthcare educators and practitioners, not only has CHD remained the leading cause of death, but Americans have grown fatter and more sedentary, and they have contracted a whole host of chronic diseases that were unknown 30 years ago, such as Epstein-Barr (chronic fatigue syndrome) and fibromyalgia.

We now know that the body needs periodic bouts of physical stress to maintain a proper level of health in every physiological system, including the cardiovascular, immune system, nervous, and digestive systems. Ironically, physical exercise is a form of stress: In no uncertain terms, physical exercise is the fulfillment of the fight-or-flight response. In the course of exercise, heart rate, blood pressure, respiration, perspiration, and muscle tension all increase, and the physical demands for energy metabolism initiate a cascade of hormones and enzymes for energy production.

Physical exercise isn't the fountain of youth, but it does do something that other relaxation techniques don't do as well. Under stress, your body produces a flood of stress hormones, including cortisol, vasopressin, and aldosterone. Because these same hormones are produced during exercise, they are used for their intended purpose rather than causing ultimate wear and tear on the body. Furthermore, upon the completion of your workout, exercise acts to flush these hormones out of the body. Perhaps the best effect of exercise is what is known as the parasympathetic rebound effect: After exercise, your heart rate, blood pressure, and breathing cycles return to a lower resting rate than before you exercised. In a day and age when physical threats are few and far between, the actual need to run or fight may seem rather antiquated, but nothing could be further from the truth. Mental, emotional, and spiritual stressors have replaced physical stressors, and although you cannot physically run away from these problems, cardiovascular exercise has proven to be a valuable means to deal with these kinds of problems as well. Simply by bringing the body back into balance (homeostasis), the other wellness components are positively affected.

Over the past several decades, fitness and exercise programs have had many makeovers in an effort to cross the threshold of people's boredom level and thoughts of exercise as work: aerobics, Jazzercise, spinning, water aerobics, Pilates, PLYOGA (Pilates and yoga), and more recently CrossFit training. We can expect to see more makeovers over time, but the basics of cardiovascular and neuromuscular exercise won't change. Find a workout style that you like best, and make it part of your daily routine.

Energy Balance

It is hard to walk by the checkout stand at the local grocer and not notice the latest fad diet grabbing the headlines. Low protein, high protein, low carb, low fat, high density, low toxins, low calories—the list is long and frequently changes. Quite frankly, there is no one diet for everyone, and research reveals that diets have a rather poor success rate. This much we know about diets: To maintain your weight, the number of calories consumed must equal the number of calories expended.

Weight loss results from less calories eaten than expended, and weight gain results from more calories eaten than burned. This is the science behind what is referred to as **energy balance**. The body, in all its amazing wonder and wisdom, knows enough to store calories that may be needed later for fight or flight.

Another simple truth is that excess carbohydrates which are not metabolized into glucose and used for energy are stored as fat (adipose tissue, or what some people refer to as cellulite). Moreover, protein that is not used for refurbishing cell structure and other metabolic demands, such as hormone and enzyme synthesis, is also stored as fat. Lipids, including triglycerides (known as fats), that are not needed for metabolic demands are stored as adipose tissue. Given the "supersize" mentality of our fast-food nation and the sedentary lifestyle of the couch potato culture, it's no wonder that obesity is such a problem. The bottom line is that there is a huge imbalance in the energy balance.

Cortisol and Weight Gain

Is there a connection between chronic stress and obesity? Perhaps. There is new speculation that cortisol, a hormone released from the adrenal gland during the stress response, may be related to the steady accumulation of body fat in one's lifetime. Given the amount of chronic stressors each American has today, and the incredible rate of obesity, there may indeed be a connection. Cortisol is responsible for a number of metabolic activities for fight or flight, including ensuring the release of glucose and free fatty acids into the blood for short- and long-term energy. If a person chooses not to fight or flee (anaerobic or aerobic exercise), watching hours of television instead, then the body may redistribute these energy nutrients as adipose tissue (fat). Additional speculation suggests that cortisol may be a principle hormone to regulate appetite under stress, to ensure that there is an adequate supply of both short- and long-term energy. It is well known that stress (acute and chronic) raises blood sugar levels of type 2 diabetics, hence making an exercise program all the more important for this particular population.

A training program that includes regular cardiovascular exercise helps to ensure that the hormones synthesized and released as a result of chronic stress are used for their intended purpose and then flushed out of the system with other metabolic waste products. Exercise also burns calories, making this a desired health package for everyone. It's no secret that the marketplace is becoming flooded with drugs and herbal products intended to minimize or block the effect of cortisol on appetite and weight gain. However, drugs and supplements can have any number of side effects, throwing your body's biochemistry out of balance. When performed correctly, the short- and long-term effects of exercise restore balance to mind, body, and spirit with no harmful side effects—and it's free.

The Mind-Body-Spirit Connection

From cereal boxes to infomercials, physical exercise is promoted as the best way to maintain physical fitness. Although this is quite true, a whole other side to exercise receives far less notoriety, yet it is equally important: the impact of exercise, specifically cardiovascular exercise, on the mind. Ask anyone who has maintained a cardiovascular fitness program for any length of time, and they will tell you that what first began as a fitness regime soon became a mental health program. Rhythmic activities such as running, swimming, walking, or bike riding not only allow for emotional catharsis but also become a type of meditation. The continuous deep breathing cycle, repetitive physical motion, or perhaps both act as a mantra for increased concentration and awareness, thus giving the mind a sense of peace. With greater mental clarity comes greater access to right-brain cognitive skills, making imagination, acceptance, receptivity, intuition, and other right-brain functions highly accessible and making an aerobic activity session truly a holistic modality.

There are additional benefits. When the term *runner's high* was first coined, nonrunners thought this was a marketing strategy to win them over. It took science a while to catch up with psychology, but evidence now reveals that the brain produces a series of neurochemicals, or neuropeptides, that have an opiate-like quality. Beta-endorphin was found to be the primary chemical agent that produced a euphoric sensation when running, swimming, walking, or performing any other activity with the proper intensity, frequency, and duration.

How to Incorporate Physical Exercise into Your Life Routine

In simple terms, there are two types of exercise: *anaerobic* and *aerobic*. Although these terms have become household words to some, a quick review is useful. Anaerobic exercise involves short, intense bursts of energy that typically last no longer than a few minutes, usually less. Because the supplies of blood and oxygen are deficient, muscle contractions are the result of stored energy in the muscle by way of the chemical compound adenosine diphosphate (ADP). The word *aerobic* means "in the presence of oxygen," and the energy demands from this type of work require oxygen, delivered by the blood, for muscle contraction. Because the redistribution of blood from the body's core (GI tract) to the periphery (arms and legs) takes about 5 minutes, the first part of an aerobic workout involves some anaerobic work.

Examples of anaerobic work include weight lifting, sprints, and isometric exercises. Aerobic exercise, also referred to as cardio exercise, includes jogging, walking, swimming, cycling, spinning, and any other activity during which the supply of oxygen meets the demand of the work involved. Using a stress metaphor, anaerobic work is used in the fight response, whereas aerobic work is employed in the flight response.

To incorporate physical exercise into your life routine, begin by setting some reasonable goals for yourself. Do you wish to lose some (fat) weight? Do you wish to lower your resting heart rate and blood pressure? Perhaps you would like to decrease the percentage of your body fat and increase some muscle tone, or maybe you wish to celebrate your 30th, 40th, or 50th birthday by deciding to run a 10K road race or a marathon. Select a reasonable goal, decide what type of exercise (aerobic or anaerobic) is best suited for this goal, and then begin to map out a workout strategy to help you accomplish this goal. Determine the right components for fitness (read the all-or-none principle in the next section) as well as ways to chart your progress. Remember that some goals may require you to seek a trained professional coach (e.g., a marathon coach). Remember to start small and slow and work your way up to a greater challenge. Ideally, a well-balanced or holistic exercise program includes a combination of both anaerobic work (muscle strength) and aerobic work (cardiovascular endurance). Exercises 7.1 and 7.2 can assist you in putting together a cardiovascular fitness program.

The All-or-None Conditioning Principle

It's no secret that laziness is a force to be reckoned with in the American lifestyle. Given the chance, most people would rather sit and rest than get up and exercise. Mark Twain once said, "Whenever I get the urge to exercise, I lie down until the feeling passes away." Sadly, his thought on this matter is not unique. Perhaps for this reason, researchers in the field of exercise physiology have studied the dynamics of exercise to determine what is the minimal amount required to gain the coveted health benefits. The dynamics involved include four factors of exercise: intensity, frequency, duration, and mode. To gain the benefits of exercise, one must employ all of these or receive none of the benefits, hence the name **all-or-none conditioning principle**.

- *Intensity:* Intensity is the challenge placed on the specific physiological system being worked (e.g., cardiovascular, musculoskeletal). Intensity of exercise is typically expressed as one's target heart rate for cardiovascular work (75 percent of one's maximal heart rate), whereas pounds, reps, and sets are used to determine the level of intensity for muscle strength.
- *Frequency:* Frequency is determined by the number of workouts per week. The minimum recommended number of workouts per week is three, with usually a day of rest between each workout.
- *Duration:* Duration is measured by the amount of time spent exercising. The minimum duration per workout is 20–30 minutes if you add a 5-minute warm-up and a 5-minute cool down.
- *Mode:* Different types of exercise are designed to challenge different physiological systems. Weight training will not enhance one's cardiovascular endurance very well, nor will jogging develop muscle strength, although it will help tone muscles. The mode of exercise is specific for the benefits you wish to gain.

Phases of a Workout

Regardless of which mode of exercise you choose to do, experts agree that every workout should follow the progression of these three steps:

1. *Warm-up:* A period of 5–10 minutes during which blood flow is allowed to redistribute to the large muscle groups, followed by light stretching. When you start breaking a sweat, then a proper warm-up has been achieved.
2. *Stimulus period:* A period of 20 minutes (or more) during which the intensity of the activity is reached and maintained for the duration of the exercise period.
3. *Cool down:* A 5- to 10-minute period of decreased intensity that allows for a gradual shift in the flow of blood from the large muscle groups to the body's core. Most exercise physiologists insist that this is as crucial as the stimulus period, because without a proper cool down, complications with the cardiovascular system may arise.

A Word About Soreness and Injuries

In exercise circles, there are two kinds of pain: good pain and bad pain. Good pain (dull pain) occurs when muscles are sore, but the soreness comes from the lack of use and typically disappears within hours to a day or so. Bad pain (sharp pain) is a sensation generated from the joints and doesn't lessen in a few hours. Sprains, strains, and fractures fall in the bad-pain category and may require medical attention.

Additional Tips for a Successful Exercise Program

- *Start cautiously and progress moderately with your exercise routine.* The biggest problem with exercise programs is when people do too much too soon, resulting in injuries. For this reason, sage advice reminds us to start slow and work our way up to the routine we wish to maintain. Most people begin exercise programs not to keep their heart or bones healthy but to lose weight. Although exercise is a great means to lose weight, the simple truth is that pounds don't disappear overnight. The recommended speed of weight loss, so that it stays off, is about 1–2 pounds per week. Typically anything more than this is water loss, which will return with rehydration.
- *Select an activity you really enjoy.* Because obesity is such a concern in the American population (not to mention CHD), the focus of attention is on cardiovascular exercise—and for good reason. The good news is that there are many different types of cardiovascular exercise, including walking. It's best to pick an activity that you like or think you like and begin with that. It's also important to have a backup activity in the event that an injury prevents you from continuing or you simply get bored with the sport. Most people quit their exercise programs out of boredom, so variety is also a good aspect to consider.
- *Select a specific time of day to exercise.* A routine is essential for maintaining a healthy exercise program. Selecting a specific time each day to exercise (even if you only do it three times per week) creates healthy boundaries. Some people consider exercise a lower priority than work and, hence, when work piles up the workout gets canceled at a time when it's probably most important. Establish healthy boundaries with your exercise routine and stick to it.
- *Exercise with the best clothes and equipment.* You don't have to spend a lot of money for exercise equipment (although many people do). Perhaps the most important piece of equipment is a good pair of workout shoes. Although spending $100 on a pair of running shoes may seem outrageous, consider that a pair of good shoes is really an insurance policy against injuries. It's worth the extra money to ensure that you don't get hurt during a workout. If you begin to get sharp joint pain, the first thing to consider is a new pair of exercise shoes.
- *Initiate an exercise support group.* Let's face it: Exercise is work, and it's easy to quit work when you're working out by yourself. It's harder to back out when you have made a commitment with others to do it together. Working out with a friend makes the time go by more quickly, and camaraderie can be a great motivation to stay with your program. If you are having a hard time getting or staying motivated, consider inviting some friends to join you.

- *Set personal fitness goals for yourself.* Even the best exercise routines can become monotonous without a goal to reach. Some people use road races as personal goals. Others set personal health goals (e.g., lower cholesterol, lower resting heart rate). Having a personal goal serves as great intrinsic motivation to get out of the house when other things seem to distract you from exercising.
- *Take care and prevent injuries.* An injury can become a stressor quite quickly. If you are using exercise to reduce stress, this is the last thing you want to happen. If you feel joint soreness at any time during exercise, stop. If you feel general soreness after a workout (this is to be expected), give yourself a day's rest before exercising again.

Your Body's Natural Rhythms

Your body runs on a natural biological clock. Science calls this clock your **circadian rhythm,** and it has been the topic of much interest over the past hundred years. We know that the body craves not only exercise and relaxation but also a routine schedule. Apparently, changes (big or small) in eating, sleeping, engaging in physical exercise, and other lifestyle habits tend to throw off your circadian rhythm. When this is thrown off, your health suffers, sometimes dramatically. Exercise 7.3 invites you to check in with your circadian rhythm to determine whether it promotes or detracts from your health status.

In the midst of experiencing chronic pain, the last thing you may wish to do is exercise, but some types of exercise may in fact be the best thing for you. Overtraining in any sport, whether it be running, cycling, or swimming, can lead to an overuse syndrome, which can precipitate chronic joint or muscle pain. Physical exercise can exaggerate a difference in leg length or knee stability issues. One type of exercise that may indeed help chronic pain is Pilates. Developed by Joseph Pilates early in the 20th century as a series of exercises to strengthen the core muscles of the body's frame, Pilates was originally used by dancers and athletes for both prevention and rehabilitation of athletic injuries. Today, like hatha yoga, Pilates classes are commonly taught at fitness clubs and Pilates centers around the country.

Developing Your Mastery of Exercise as a Relaxation Technique

Exercise as a relaxation technique is one of the best ways to bring balance back into your life. Walking is the most underrated activity, and nearly everyone can walk. Any other sports require some skill, yet skills increase with practice. Although the benefits of a single bout of exercise can be felt almost immediately, research shows that it takes about 6–8 weeks to notice more significant changes, such as weight loss, decreased cholesterol, and so on. To really gain the full effects of physical exercise, your exercise routine must be as much a part of your life as taking a shower and brushing your teeth.

Best Benefits of Physical Exercise

If you could take all the benefits of physical exercise and manufacture them in a pill, it would be the most popular pharmaceutical in the world—but you cannot. Our bodies were designed for exercise. They were not designed to sit in front of a computer screen all day or a television all night. Physical exercise is actually good stress for the body; the body requires it to keep things in balance. By not exercising, the cardiovascular system becomes less efficient, bones begin to demineralize, energy balance is compromised, and several other metabolic processes become unbalanced.

The benefits of exercise have to be gained from the actual work of exercise, and exercise is work, but the payoffs are incredible.

Following is a short list of the beneficial effects of regular exercise:

- Increased immune system function
- Increased quality of sleep
- Decreased resting heart rate and blood pressure
- Increased mental alertness and concentration skills
- Slowing of the aging process

Chapter Summary

- Physical exercise is stress to the body, but in proper amounts, it is good stress that the body needs to maintain a healthy balance for optimal living.
- Physical exercise helps regulate one's energy balance.
- The stress hormone cortisol is associated with weight gain; exercise can help regulate cortisol.
- Exercise may be good for the body, but it's also good for the mind, from helping to induce the "runner's high" to creative problem solving.
- For exercise to be beneficial, it must include the right aspects of intensity, frequency, and duration.
- A proper exercise routine must include an adequate warm-up, stimulus period, and cool-down period.
- Your body's 24-hour "clock" is known as your circadian rhythm. For optimal healthy living, it is suggested to eat, sleep, and exercise at about the same time every day to honor this rhythm.

Additional Resources

Anderson, B. *Stretching*, 30th Anniversary Edition. Bolinas, CA: Shelter; 2010.

Andreas, S. *Cross Training and Paleo: The Beginner's Guide*, Kindle Edition. Amazon Digital Services; 2015.

Bingham, J. *No Need for Speed: A Beginner's Guide to the Joy of Running*. Emmaus, PA: Rodale Press; 2002.

Green, B. *Get with the Program*. New York, NY: Simon & Schuster; 2002.

Kowalchik, C. *The Complete Book of Running for Women*. New York, NY: Pocket; 1999.

Meyers, C. *Walking: A Complete Guide to the Complete Exercise*. New York, NY: Ballantine; 2007.

Pelletier, K. *The Best Alternative Medicine*. New York, NY: Touchstone; 2002.

Ratey, J. *Spark: The Revolutionary New Science of Exercise and the Brain*. New York, NY: Little, Brown & Co.; 2013.

Reynolds, G. *The First 20 Minutes: Surprising Science Reveals How We Can Exercise Better, Train Smarter, Live Longer*. New York, NY: Plume; 2013.

Rowe, F. *Walking Your Way to Fitness*, Kindle Edition. Amazon Digital Services; 2015.

Ten Quick Tips for Staying Grounded

Sound Strategies and Quick Tips for Adaptation and Resiliency in a Rapidly and Dramatically Changing World

KEY TERMS

Chronic stress
Creativity
Good vibes

Resiliency
Self-care
Self-compassion

There are many arduous tests in life, but few have proved to be so trying for so many people as the COVID-19 pandemic that began in 2020 and continued into 2021, with medical experts predicting that the reverberations of this global crisis will last for years, perhaps decades. From initial government lockdowns and social isolation to canceled Olympic Games and truncated professional and collegiate sports seasons, high school graduation ceremonies, summer concert series, and scores of closed favorite restaurants, followed by social distancing, face masks, and pleas to stay at home during the second and third waves of the pandemic, people from all walks of life and demographics have experienced a new normal—and not a very hospitable one. Moreover, the pandemic revealed a slew of social problems and ills that, neglected for years if not decades, reached a boiling point: Intolerable racial and economic disparities, not to mention fist fights and standoffs about wearing face masks, also made themselves known, adding to already mounting frustrations, tensions, and anxieties, as well as a few conspiracies.

Like a Category 5 hurricane that spawns devastating tornadoes, this coronavirus pandemic created a subsequent pandemic of stress, and not just in the United States but across the world. The initial run on toilet paper almost seems comical now when compared to what has happened. The American Psychological Association (APA), which conducts an annual study titled "Stress in America," a pulse-check on the current stress climate, quickly realized that one study for 2020 wasn't enough. Instead the APA has conducted three studies with a fourth in the works. Topping the list of stressors begging attention for resolution is the stress associated with politics and the lack of leadership. Moreover, there is both a growing sense of social anxiety, coupled with COVID fatigue, creating an environment ripe for a colossal mental health crisis.

Experts from a number of different disciplines suggest, even predict, that as our world spins further into the 21st century we will face new crises and problems with uncertain impacts and outcomes from the COVID-19 pandemic that will affect everyone. This is all the more reason why having a personal **resiliency** strategy is essential for optimal wellness. There is no doubt that troubling times like these can bring out our real selves. Yet, where there is fear, there is also hope and triumph. While some people choose to wear the armor of anger and fear, others take the high road and become role models of compassion in action for us all. This is not the first time a catastrophic event has forced people to pivot and adapt to sudden and subsequent change, nor will it be the last. The sooner we learn to ground and center ourselves, the better we will be at adapting to current and future waves of social and personal stress

Human beings are remarkably resilient. How we choose to respond to these challenges will prove to be our greatest asset or liability. A great mantra that underscores the premise of positive behavior change goes like this: *To know and not to do is not to know.* It means that we can know all the right things to do to make our lives less stressful, but if we don't do them, what good are they? This chapter invites you to learn, perhaps relearn, some effective time-tested strategies that will help you to navigate the stormy waters of these changing times and to do so with grace and aplomb.

In these crazy times of change we need to be able to change, and to do so quickly. Being able to pivot without losing our balance is one of the first steps in staying above the fray. Learning to adapt to the winds of change rather than fighting these same winds is one of the keys to resiliency. Resiliency has been studied by a great many people trying to figure out the formula for success in dire times. As it turns out, there is no magic or alchemical formula, nor any specific characteristic that makes someone resilient to the winds of change because everyone is different, stressors are different, and these two aspects make defining a formula impossible. We do know that resiliency, the ability to bounce back from a bad situation, isn't a gift for a chosen few. It is a birthright for everyone. We can all learn to become more resilient, but it is a skill that takes much practice.

The following suggestions are time-tested strategies and surefire tips to help you create a personal strategy for resiliency and the tools for personal adaptation in these rapidly and dramatic times. Please consider adopting (and adapting) one or more of these into your personal wellness (and stress relief) program.

Tip 1: Establish a Routine

Any type of stressor can throw one off of one's typical routine. The collective stress from the COVID-19 pandemic has proved this many times over (so much so, that people have sometimes been at a loss for what day it is: Oh yeah, it's Blursday!). When simple routines are lost, the boundaries to contain our lives become unorganized, dismantled, and sometimes vanished into thin air. Perhaps the most important step in regaining a sense of control in the face of any crisis is to reestablish specific routines to provide a sense of stability in your life.

There is great comfort in the known, and as we have seen there are countless unknowns with this pandemic event. Fear of the unknown creates a lot of stress. Having a routine reinforces the known, and that can certainly bring a sense of peace of mind. Take a moment to reflect on your personal routine over the past several months. Are you still wearing pajamas all day long? Are you stuck eating the same meals every evening for dinner? Sketch out your typical day: Start with mealtimes, meditation times, time in nature (see Tip 2), personal time (this is definitely different from your work-from-home time), and time with others. Remember to be flexible with all routines. Being rigid can lead to unmet expectations, frustrations, and hence more stress. At the same time, be firm enough with your routines that you don't assume the role of victim. This too only leads to more stress. Remember the expression "Once a victim, twice a volunteer." Establish a few routines and do your best to stick with them.

When social workers and therapists arrived in New Orleans after Hurricane Katrina, they noticed that some people clearly needed a lot of help getting back on their feet, whereas others were already making headway in putting their lives back together. One of the personal strategies that the second group had in common was that they had established a daily routine to create some order out of the chaos that resulted from the devastating storm.

Establishing a routine creates a sense of normalcy when your world has been turned upside down, when what was once considered normal is gone and a new normal is needed. Establishing a new personal routine lies at the foundation of returning to a new normal. Again, remember that while having a routine is great, a little variety (flexibility) is also a good idea.

To help you build your power of adaptation and resiliency try Exercise 8.1–8.4.

Stress with a Human Face

When the pandemic hit and canceled school in her town, sending kids home to online learning programs, Jenn felt the earth move under her feet like a California earthquake, but with months of aftershocks. Not only were she and her husband forced to work from home now, but three kids were also home, all trying to use two computers. Like horses running free out of the stable, the first few days were crazy. Then Jenn grabbed the reins and pulled hard to gain control of a situation about to get totally out of control. She explained it to me this way: "These are the new rules," she told her family, and then she proceeded to explain a new routine for all of them to follow, specifically the use of the home computers and schedules for the use of the dining room table. This also included the best times for grocery shopping, dog walks, and mealtimes.

Initially, Jenn stripped down everything to the essentials. Once that was established and in place, Jenn introduced some additional routines, like supervised sports activities and enrichment programs for the kids and personal time for herself. By the time the second wave of the pandemic hit months later, Jenn's household was ready for more home schooling. Big changes didn't rock the boat like they did before. And that has made all the difference.

Tip 2: Practice Nature Therapy

Within weeks of the COVID-19 lockdown, people began to understand firsthand the experience of "cabin fever." As spring turned into summer, fish and game authorities across the country noted a dramatic increase in fishing license applications. Bike store owners couldn't keep up with restocking their inventory. Once the national parks reopened, the demand for park passes surpassed what had been requested for years before the pandemic. Parks and recreational areas were packed with people. Kids were playing in the streets, not glued to their video games. Something had changed. If there is one thing the coronavirus pandemic has taught the world, it's that you cannot stay cooped up in your house or apartment all day for months on end as if you are under house arrest. Getting some fresh air and sunshine is essential to your health.

Entire days may disappear while surfing the Internet, and this poor time-management strategy will only create more chaos in your life. As such, make a concerted effort (make time) to get outside each day, even if it's in your own backyard (see **Figure 8.1**). Remember: Your home should be a place of comfort, not a prison. Go for a 20-minute walk around the neighborhood or a local park, if possible. If not, no worries, but either way consider filling your backyard bird feeders. Make an effort to get in touch with nature. Know what phase the moon is in and get outside to view it. Feel sunlight on your face (get some vitamin D, knowing that it's deemed essential for your immune system). Breathe in the fresh spring air, the summer breezes, and watch the autumn leaves falling to the ground. Reacquaint yourself with the smell of spring rain. Listen to the birds sing (mating calls), the calls of owls, and spend some time each day in a garden of your own making (get your hands dirty with garden soil). If you can afford it, purchase a house plant (and talk to it—they love that) or propagate a plant you already have. Before you go to bed, step outside and end the evening looking

Figure 8.1 Make time to get out in nature and connect with the natural world.

for a new constellation (the "Night Sky" app is great for this). If you cannot make it outside every day, watch a great online nature video, such as *Earth Songs: The Healing Power of Nature*. And if it is impossible to go outside, go inside (see Tip 9: Meditate Daily!).

To help you build your power of adaptation and resiliency, try Exercise 8.5.

Stress with a Human Face

Before the pandemic, Todd spent too much of his time glued to his screen device, mostly out of boredom, sometimes curiosity, but the large percentage of screen time was wasted time. When he heard an episode on NPR's *Fresh Air* about how important vitamin D is to one's health, particularly the immune system, he took this as a wake-up call and decided to make some changes in his new pandemic lifestyle and get outside. Dusting off an old passion for photography that he first nurtured in college, Todd decided to dive into the world of nature, capturing moments of the natural world with a real camera (not his smartphone, which he left at home). He first started taking morning walks at sunrise (known in photography circles as the golden hour) in a nature preserve near his house. It was there he saw and photographed great horned owls, white-tailed deer, wild coyotes, foxes, and scores of waterfowl, as well as some incredible sunrises. Within a few weeks, he decided to head to a local nursery and purchase some flowers and plants that would attract hummingbirds to his backyard. Within days of planting, the hummingbirds arrived, turning his backyard into a menagerie of winged delight. Todd didn't stop there. From a group of photographers in his local area, he learned of some of their favorite spots to photograph black bears, bobcats, and even moose. Todd was in heaven. Within weeks, even his wife noticed a remarkable difference in Todd's attitude. He was happy. Time in nature made him forget about all the social ills and lost freedoms that the pandemic imposed. Even if all he could do was spend time in his backyard, his newfound natural connection became a prescription for optimal wellness.

Tip 3: Nurture and Honor Your Support Groups

If the COVID pandemic has taught us anything, it is the importance of family, friends, and the need for support from peers, colleagues, and neighbors. Family, friends, and neighbors are all essential members of our support network. Remember: No one is an island—we are all a part of community. Make it a point to take time to reach out (virtually or by phone) to your friends and family, not only to check up on each other but also to remind yourself that you belong to a group, a tribe. Don't let social isolation cut you off from your tribe. Quarantines can reinforce feelings of isolation and alienation, and these feelings can be precursors for emotional stress, specifically depression. Both alienation and isolation were serious health issues before the pandemic. They have only become more so now. Support groups (real or virtual) make it safe to ask for help, and in these times we all need to help each other. If you need help, ask for it without shame or embarrassment.

Moreover, if you can lend a hand, do so. Practicing the Golden Rule is a cornerstone of support groups (formal ones like Al-Anon, or informal ones). Yes, we must all practice social distancing, but people have quickly adapted. Previous pandemics left people in extreme situations. This pandemic is different in part because we have the Internet with FaceTime visits, Facebook video chats, Zoom calls, and emails. Even old-fashioned letter writing and phone calls work to keep us connected. Unless you're a monk with a meditation practice high in the Himalayan mountains, make it a point to connect with at least one person a day.

To help you create and nurture a stronger support system in these challenging times, please try Exercise 8.6.

Stress with a Human Face

Long before COVID-19 (or even SARS and Ebola), Sara started attending Al-Anon support group meetings once she realized that her first husband had a drinking problem. More than looking for answers to her troubled marriage, Sara found people to whom she could relate—she simply enjoyed the company of others working through a similar situation. Several years ago, she divorced her husband but kept going to the support group meetings because she loved the camaraderie, as well as the guidance and structure of a 12-Step program. Moreover, she decided that she too had an addiction—an addiction to food—and so she began to attend meetings of Overeaters Anonymous, a support group for that. When the COVID-19 pandemic set in, the weekly in-person meetings moved online. Sara confided that online group meetings are not as good for her as the in-person ones, but her support groups mean everything to her, so she attended online.

Sara also confided in another type of support. Being very close with her two sisters and mother (her father had passed away many years ago), yet unable to see each other month after month, Sara started a weekly family Zoom chat. Even her mother, who was a self-described dinosaur when it came to technology, figured out how to join the get-together. In the summer of 2020, few restaurants were open to meet in person for a family gathering, so Sara arranged a food pick-up service and organized a Zoom-style dinner party, and this tradition, she says, will be continued as long as it is needed.

Tip 4: Practice Creative Anger Management

These can be incredibly frustrating times. Many freedoms have been denied, and with frustrations come more stress. Remember: Every episode of anger or frustration is the result of an unmet expectation. In these times, there are plenty of unmet expectations to go around: canceled concerts, canceled vacations, closed restaurants, face-mask regulations, required COVID tests, size limits for groups and gatherings—the list grows daily. It is important to remember that anger (like fear), as a survival emotion, is a healthy emotion, but only in tiny amounts. If anger persists, you end up giving your power away and become controlled by your anger. Anger that persists is also known as a control drama, fueled by the ego. If you find yourself getting angry, it is best to stop for a moment and ask yourself why. Why are you angry? What are you angry about? What expectation wasn't met? Do you have any influence on the outcome? Mostly likely not. If so, let it go. Remember the expression "He or she who angers you conquers you." Don't let your emotions conquer you.

Managing your anger creatively involves first recognizing your feelings and how you are reacting to the unmet expectation. Next, creative anger management involves resolving (making peace with) the issue and moving on. In some cases, creative anger management requires stepping away (time-outs) to cool off. In other cases, it means deactivating your "buttons" (triggers) so that when other people push them, you don't react and give your power away. Remember: In a time when everyone seems angry, this emotional energy too becomes a contagious virus. Learn to inoculate yourself against the vitriol of others by taking the high road, staying above the fray, and not taking on someone else's stress as your own.

Healthy anger involves healthy grieving too. Healthy grieving means acknowledging a personal loss (often the loss of an expectation), acknowledging the feelings surrounding it, and then doing your best to let it go. Sometimes it helps to talk about it with others. Remember: It's never healthy to keep such feelings in because in doing so they become toxic. Keeping toxic feelings in (suppressing them) tends to suppress the immune system, and given the times we are in, this is *not* a good idea.

To help you learn to creatively manage your anger feelings, please try Exercise 8.7–8.11.

Stress with a Human Face

If you knew Marty, you wouldn't think of him as an angry person, but that was before February 2020. A canceled safari vacation to South Africa; several canceled conferences, rock concerts, and baseball games; closed restaurants, bars, and national parks; basically the loss of his normal life had become too much, or so he thought. The loss of his normal life became too much, or so he thought. Marty saw his life change drastically before his eyes and lost his grip emotionally. As the expression goes, he flew off the handle about everything, from political ads on TV to rude drivers on the road. He lost his temper regularly with his girlfriend, his parents, his employees, even his dog. It was his girlfriend who gave him the ultimatum: Get help or get out.

Faced with the choice of losing more than his friends and business, Marty got some counseling. It was there he learned that his anger was the result of unhealthy grieving (in his case, it was the death of the old normal). With some good counseling and some new coping skills, he learned to cope (grieve) with the death of expectations. Marty regained some composure around his frustration, angst, and, most important, conversations with family and friends. In a few short weeks, he turned his life around. He even volunteered to help others with their anger outbursts. When the second wave of COVID-19 hit, Marty was ready. He had a new set of coping skills to deal with stress. What is the biggest lesson he learned from all of this? "Not to give your power away," he said. "So much of stress management is not giving your power (emotions) away to things beyond your control. Once I realized that, life under the pandemic became a lot more manageable."

Tip 5: Establish/Practice Healthy Boundaries

Routines (Tip 1) are important, but healthy boundaries are essential. Declaring personal time (in a crowded space) is essential. Sleep behaviors, eating behaviors, financial behaviors, screen-time behaviors all demand healthy boundaries. The expression "healthy boundaries" is code for appropriate behaviors. Without good boundaries, life seems chaotic. Chaos in times of crisis only leads to more chaos, which is all the more reason to establish healthy boundaries. In simple terms, there are three kinds of behavior: passive, aggressive, and assertive. Establishing healthy boundaries is an act of assertive behavior. In essence, it is pulling up the welcome mat so people don't walk over you. Healthy boundaries are also a lesson in self-control where you balance personal freedom with responsibilities. Not having good boundaries in your life opens you up to seeing yourself as a victim, and this thought process leads to more stress. Done correctly, healthy boundaries can prove to be liberating. In what may seem like an oxymoron, by establishing healthy boundaries you give yourself the freedom to stop being manipulated by others and becoming the victim of your lack of willpower. Like a cell membrane that regulates what comes in and what stays outside of the cell, healthy boundaries offer both structure and flexibility.

Where in your life do you need to make a course correction? Where in your life (e.g., eating habits, screen-time habits, sleep habits, exercise habits, financial habits, relationships) can you begin to pull on the reins so you don't feel like you are riding a wild horse off a cliff?

If it helps, write down a few of your healthy boundaries. You may need to communicate these to others you live with and ask or remind them to honor these as well. One suggestion: Limit time you spend on social media and network news. Follow up each week to review your boundaries.

Again, adopting a consciousness of victimization is not the way to go. See each healthy boundary as a personal course correction toward where you wish to see yourself in the days ahead. Establishing healthy boundaries is a skill, and skills take practice. The more you practice them, the better you become with them.

To help you create some healthy boundaries in your life, try Exercise 8.12.

Stress with a Human Face

Even before the COVID-19 pandemic turned life upside down, Charlie's life could best be described as a train wreck. His wife left him. He lost his job. His car was repossessed. He was denied custody of his three children. A low credit rating denied him the chance to get a suitable apartment to live in.

All hope seemed lost when he stumbled upon a stress management seminar and learned about healthy boundaries. At first he snickered at the concept. But eventually the term *healthy boundaries* became a mantra for him. Within 6 months, he set some new boundaries as a course correction for his life. In this stage, with the help of healthy boundaries, he got his life back on track and became the captain of his fate. In early spring 2020, when people were freaking out in regard to pandemic lockdowns and face masks, Charlie was calm, cool, and collected. By the time the pandemic hit hard, healthy boundaries were a big asset for Charlie. Already familiar with the concept, Charlie put additional healthy boundaries to work regarding screen time (a new media curfew at 8:30 p.m.) and no snacks during the day (to avoid the "COVID-20" gain in pounds). As the second wave of the coronavirus caused more illness, deaths, lockdowns, business closures, and canceled events, Charlie remained unfazed. He knew that with freedom comes responsibility, and with healthy boundaries comes freedom.

Tip 6: Finding Comic Relief: Working Your Funny Bone

How is your sense of humor these days? In these crazy times, we all need to work our funny bone. In the research regarding resiliency, a sense of humor is one of the critical factors associated with being resilient, which experts agree is essential to coping with stress. It is *that* important. So, how *is* your sense of humor these days?

It is important to remember that humor isn't an emotion. Humor, like stress, is a perception. (How many times have you told what you thought was the funniest joke and no one laughed?) A humorous perception can certainly ease stress and tension, particularly when we learn to make light of ourselves and our own mistakes. Self-deprecating humor is the highest form of humor therapy.

Humor researchers remind us that humor is a complex phenomenon. Types of humor include satire, parody, slapstick, absurd humor, dry humor, black humor, puns, double entendres, irony, and, of course, bathroom humor. There is also sarcasm, an anger-based humor that is the lowest form of humor and one not recommended. Remember: The word *sarcasm* means "to tear flesh."

In all times, but particularly in these chaotic times, be on the lookout for some comic relief. Try to find one funny thing each day. Become your own best audience. Social media is overflowing with funny memes, videos, and jokes, running the gambit from black humor to irony to double and triple entendres. Consider collecting the best of all of these and make a tickler notebook. Your sense of humor will prove to be one of your greatest assets in these changing times. If it helps, remember that the word *humor* means "fluid" or "moisture," a constant reminder to go with the flow.

To help you nurture your sense of comic relief (and support your resilient nature), try Exercise 8.13.

Stress with a Human Face

When the pandemic hit and forced a series of lockdowns, social distancing, and loads of time to contemplate life, Tom realized he had two choices: (1) get stuck in the negativity (which there was plenty of) or (2) look for the funny side of it all and laugh. He chose the latter. He quickly discovered that there was much to laugh at about the pandemic, particularly on social media. "The amount of black humor was amazing." As Tom's friends will tell you, he has always had a great sense of humor. The COVID-19 pandemic just brought out more of it. In fact, his friends say he is his own best audience—he is always laughing at something. Sometimes when he tells a joke, the joke itself is nowhere near as funny as Tom laughing when he tells it. Whatever you do, don't hand him a glass of milk before he tells a joke, unless you want to see a human version of Niagara Falls come out of his nose. What are some of his favorite pandemic jokes or chuckles? Here are a few:

Quarantine: Day 1
Man with coronavirus seeks woman with Lyme disease.

Quarantine: Day 9
My wife called from the other room and asked if I ever get a stabbing pain in my chest, like someone has a voodoo doll of me and is stabbing it.
    I replied, "No."
    She responded, "How about now?"

Quarantine: Day 14
My hubby purchased a world map on Amazon, gave me a dart, and said, "Throw this, and wherever it lands, I'm taking you there for a holiday when this pandemic is over."
    Turns out we're spending two weeks behind the fridge.

Quarantine: Day 20
When this virus is over I still want some of you to stay away from me.

Quarantine: Day 21
Single man with TP seeks single woman with hand sanitizer for good, clean fun.

Meme
Photo of Rod Sterling, creator of the *Twilight Zone*:
                    Even the Twilight Zone wasn't this crazy.

Meme
Photo of Betty White and Keith Richards:
    Keith Richards and Betty White escape from Earth to repopulate the species.

Meme
Photo of Planet Earth:
        2020: Written by Stephen King, Directed by Quentin Tarantino

Meme
Famous American Gothic painting:
    Farming couple inside looking out windows, abandoned pitchfork lying on the front lawn

Meme
T-shirt image of sloth in lotus position:
                Namaste . . . 6 feet away

Meme
Illustration of Yoko Ono singing on city streets to ensure New York residents stay inside

Perhaps the best meme
Michelangelo's *Last Supper* painting with Jesus by himself doing a Zoom conference with the 12 apostles. Jesus says:
                Judas, Judas, are you there?

Cartoon:
The Grim Reaper is at the front door, pushes the intercom, and says:
        It ruins the effect if I say who it is. Can you just come down?

Tip 7: Begin or End Each Day with a Gratitude List

It's hard to feel sorry for yourself when you are engaged in an attitude of gratitude, and no matter your situation, there is much for which to be grateful. In comparison to people living in less-developed countries, in North America we are doing rather well with our quality of life, even in quarantine. Remember that. As a popular meme says, "You are not stuck at home, you are safe at home." Recognize the difference, and be grateful. Americans and Canadians honor the practice of gratitude with the holiday of Thanksgiving, but don't limit yourself to just one day. Consider extending this practice every day. Often referred to as an attitude of gratitude, stopping to give thanks regularly helps put stress in perspective, and it often makes us realize that as bad as we might have it, for the most part we have it pretty good. Research shows that people who take time to consciously be grateful for various aspects of their lives not only tend to be happier than those who do not, but they also have an enhanced immune system. During any pandemic, a strong immune system is a valuable asset.

Here is a suggestion to practice on a daily basis. Identify three (3) things each day that you are appreciative of or grateful for (see **Figure 8.2**). If you cannot think of anything, begin with gratitude for breathing (unassisted by a respirator), walking, or the clean water coming out of your facet (half the world's population doesn't have this luxury). It's okay if you repeat some of these items each day.

To help you become more appreciative and grateful in these crazy times, try Exercise 8.14–8.17.

Figure 8.2 Take time each day to give thanks, particularly for the things we take for granted.

Stress with a Human Face

How do you end your day? If you were to ask Chris, she ends her day by stating three to four things she is grateful for in her life. The list is never the same. She begins with her husband (he is always at the top of the list, she says). One day her gratitude list might include having clean drinking water or a hot bath. On another day she might include having the ability to hear music (she loves the blues, particularly the style from New Orleans). One day Chris read an article online which stated that people who end their day by being thankful not only sleep better but that they have an enhanced immune system (in the age of COVID-19, this is surely an asset). In addition, becoming aware of things that make you happy reframes your thinking for you to be on the lookout for things to appreciate and be grateful for all the time. In essence, every day becomes Thanksgiving. If you are grateful, then very likely you are not stressing out about what everybody else is fretting about. Chris may end her day with an attitude of gratitude, and she begins it that way as well. A sign in her bathroom reads, "Start each day with a grateful heart."

Chris has become a fan of the work of Dr. Joe Dispenza, who has popularized the concept of neuroplasticity. Dispenza's message is to focus on positive and uplifting emotions rather than continually being stuck in the whirlpool of negativity. "Having an attitude of gratitude isn't a denial of reality," says Chris. It merely offers the option to consciously focus on the good things in life (sometimes even the bad ones and the lessons they offer), rather than constantly complaining about how bad things are. Chris was doing her bedtime gratitude list before the pandemic, and she has embraced this practice in earnest since life got turned upside down in the winter of 2020 (see **Figure 8.3**).

Figure 8.3 A word cloud made from a list of uplifting emotions.

Tip 8: Practice Creative Problem-Solving Skills

What to fix for dinner tonight? Create something new. How to re-budget your altered income? Create some options (e.g., refinance your mortgage, cook at home more rather than ordering takeout, etc.). How do you resurrect your faltering business? Have a dynamic online presence. We are all creative, and in this day and age, not only are many people going through the same situation, but many have posted on the Internet *how* they navigated around the challenges. Enlist some help to think up ideas, then try them out. **Creativity** has been studied, examined, dissected, and reimagined by everyone from Leonardo da Vinci to Steve Jobs and scores of people in between. The bottom line is that anyone can be creative. Creativity is a skill, and like all skills, it takes practice. Repeated practice. Creativity isn't a right brain function; it's a whole brain function. Sure, you need some imagination to come up with an idea, but you also need good judgment skills to see beyond the first idea, as well as good executive skills, to make a good idea happen (many a good idea never sees the light of day because the ego never lets it get past the drawing board stage.) Don't let your ego sabotage your best creative efforts.

The first step in creative problem solving is to identify the problem. The next step is to identify some options (solutions). So what are your options? As the expression goes, "A person with no options is a person in trouble." It's time to exercise your creative muscle. Think up several options, write them down, come up with a strategy (or strategies), and begin to execute them—see which ones work and then carry them out.

To help you strengthen your creative muscle and become more empowered with a sense of creativity, please try Exercise 8.18–8.19.

Stress with a Human Face

What do you do when your world is turned upside down and life as you knew it no longer exists? Basically you have two choices: You can either give up and adopt an attitude of victim consciousness, or you can grab the bull by the horns, take command of the situation, and smile as you ride off into the sunset. It was the second path that Stephanie took when the pandemic hit. She had just opened her own yoga studio, a lifelong dream, in Fort Collins, Colorado. The dream became a nightmare when she opened the doors to her new studio location only to see them close the very next day due to a statewide COVID lockdown.

Undeterred, Stephanie decided to pivot and make the best of a bad situation. The best among her options was to create an online Zoom yoga class. And that she did. With some creative marketing, a lot of cyber-footwork, and a fair amount of creative problem solving, things turned around even better than expected. Her loyal following missed the class experience, and they were eager to meet up, if only virtually. Taking her studio to a new level, Stephanie added some extra features to the class schedule, including guided meditations, laughter yoga sessions, personal yoga sessions, pranic breathing sessions, and special guest interviews. Her plan was such a success that her profits exceeded all expectations. When she was allowed to reopen, class sizes were limited due to social distancing, but Stephanie kept her online presence as well (sensing that the second wave might trigger a closure, which it did).

Tip 9: Meditate Daily!

We live in a culture of distractions. Bits and bytes of information are coming at us from all directions, and between that and all the news and social media sound bites, the effect can be dizzying, if not mind-boggling to the point of mental collapse. Yes, we have to live in this world, but we don't have to participate in the craziness of distractions. We have a choice, and the choice is to periodically unplug from the stream of sensory bombardment (some might say "Open the fire hydrant") and pause to get some mental clarity. This is the purpose of meditation: mental clarity. Coupled with this purpose is the goal to domesticate the ego, which is the source of negativity in our mind that is trigger happy pulling the fight-or-flight response alarm. A sound meditation practice hones the skill of domesticating the ego long enough to have some mental clarity to navigate your life without becoming shipwrecked on the shoals of distractions and craziness.

Figure 8.4 In these troubled times, make time to sit and collect your thoughts before your mind runs amok with distracting and fear-based thoughts.

Find (make) time each day (part of your routine and healthy boundaries) to sit quietly and focus on your breathing (see **Figure 8.4**). Put a pad of paper and pen by your side, so when distracting thoughts appear, you can quickly write them down, then close your eyes and return to putting all of your attention on your breathing. Focusing on your breathing is just one of many ways to begin and continue your meditation practice. Remember: Meditation includes many things, but first and foremost it is a means to ignore mental and emotional distractions, or it is what I commonly refer to as "domesticating the ego." Start with 5 minutes a day and build up from there. If you are new to meditation, recognize that you will get bored doing it (everyone does), and that is okay. Boredom is part of the domestication of the ego process. But stick with it. The benefits (staying grounded in the winds of change) are amazing.

To help you become more centered and grounded (and detox from digital toxicity), try Exercise 8.20.

Stress with a Human Face

Sean credits many things with keeping his sanity during the COVID-19 pandemic (even before it), but his morning meditation practice tops the list. Sean first learned the skill of meditation while on his college swim team. As he describes it, staying focused at that caliber of competition is essential. It's all about performance. Having mental discipline is not just for competitive sports. It also helps with studies and with living at home with his parents (who could stand to do some meditation as well).

Sean learned that physical training is essential for sports, but mental training is essential for life. His meditation practice starts after his morning shower. He sits for 30 minutes each day in a quiet room with no distractions (no smartphones, no people, no pets, no nothing). He begins his meditation by focusing on his breathing, just observing it: inhalations followed by exhalations. Whenever his mind wanders, he writes down the thought on a nearby pad of paper and returns to his breathing. To focus his attention, he sometimes imagines he is looking at the flame of a candle.

How has meditation helped Sean in the time of COVID? He will tell you that there is not much that rocks his boat. When he hears news that could be considered upsetting, he takes a slow, deep breath and centers his thoughts. Meditation has taught him to respond, not react. It has also helped him to sleep better too. As far as his competitive swimming goes, his teammates keep bugging him to reveal his secret to success. It's no secret—just meditation.

Tip 10: Self-Care Begins with Self-Compassion

In all the craziness and hoopla of the pandemic and all the **chronic stress** it leaves in its wake, it's important, if not essential, to take good care of yourself. Taking good care of yourself is a much advocated health and wellness behavior known as **self-care**. Self-care is so much more than finding time to take a candlelit hot bath or getting a 90-minute massage. Self-care is described as taking intentional time to nurture one's physical, mental, emotional, and spiritual health on a daily basis. Although there is no specific formula for personal self-care, there are some areas that should be addressed:

1. *Quality sleep*: Current research suggests that everyone needs 7–8 hours of quality sleep each night to function properly during the waking hours. Moreover, sleep experts agree that screen technology, of any kind, does not belong in the bedroom—this includes screens and the Wi-Fi router. Good sleep hygiene is essential for optimal functioning when awake. This means a cool, dark, quiet bedroom with ideal bedding, and a room with no distractions.

2. *Your microbiome*: We have all heard about the importance of eating well, but a healthy microbiome (our intestinal flora) is paramount to overall health and wellness. Over 70 percent of our immune system is in our microbiome. While it may be tempting to eat junk food, processed foods, and comfort foods while stuck at home, experts suggest eating at least one nutritious meal a day for your immune system (one meal, nutrient dense with vitamins and minerals.)

3. *Hydration*: Staying hydrated may seem like a simple responsibility when it comes to staying healthy, but you might be amazed to know how many people are walking around dehydrated every day. Dehydration can lead to fatigue, poor memory, poor cognitive function, low energy, and lethargy. Keeping hydrated does not include caffeinated drinks, such as coffee or energy drinks.

4. *Physical exercise*: The body craves relaxation. The body also craves a little stress. Overall, the body craves balance. It gets this balance with cardiovascular exercise. You don't have to run a marathon each day to check this box. Walking works just great. The primary purpose from a stress management perspective is to flush the stress hormones out of the body so they don't wreak havoc on your immune system. Try to get some physical exercise daily, even if it's only 15 minutes each day.

5. *Good vibes*: Lifting your spirits to make yourself feel appreciated is essential to good health. For some this might mean scheduling a full body massage. For others it might mean making a new playlist of inspiring music to listen to while making dinner or going for a walk. **Good vibes**, whether they come from music, laughter, or a good movie, are reminders to go with the flow and enjoy the ride.

6. *Self-compassion*: Self-care begins with **self-compassion**. Self-compassion is a perception of self-worth and self-appreciation which reminds you that you are worth taking time for your health. With an attitude of self-compassion, there is no guilt, no angst, and no beating yourself up when mistakes are made or goals are not met.

To help you nurture a better sense of self-care, try Exercise 8.21–8.24.

Stress with a Human Face

Andrea is a surgical nurse at a hospital in Baltimore, Maryland. Well before COVID-19 struck, she saw the handwriting on the emergency room walls. When the pandemic struck, all hell seemed to break loose in hospitals across the United States. There were not enough respirators or personal protective equipment (PPE), and all nurses were expected to shift, pivot, and adapt to provide critical care to COVID patients. Taking care of patients is nurses' primary concern. The problem with being on the front lines of the healthcare industry is that you have to make a concerted effort to do self-care. Many healthcare workers, particularly nurses, don't spend the time to do that. Andrea was determined not to let that happen. She knew the importance of getting enough sleep, eating healthy foods, and maintaining an exercise program, despite the overtime suddenly required.

When people hear the term *self-care*, they think of massages and mud baths. This was not the case for Andrea. Her self-care began with a concerted effort to practice *self-compassion*, a term she learned from reading a book with the same title, *Self-Compassion* by Kristin Neff.

Additional Resources

Note: All weblinks were accessed on October 29, 2020.

Albarelli, S. Quiet the Noise, Soothe Your Soul with Mindfulness and Meditation. TEDxYouth@ Chatham, June 2019. https://www.ted.com/talks/shannon_albarelli_quiet_the_noise_soothe_ your_soul_with_mindfulness_and_meditation.

American Management Association: Creativity and Problem Solving. January 24, 2019. https:// www.amanet.org/articles/creativity-and-problem-solving.

Davidson, R. How Mindfulness Changes the Emotional Life of Our Brains.TEDxSan Francisco. 2019. https://video.search.yahoo.com/yhs/search?fr=yhs-Lkry-SF01&hsimp=yhs-SF01&hspart =Lkry&p=TEDTalk+on+meditaiton#id=10&vid=d42890b8e2369e196740e9ab81e4e78c&act ion=view.

Drinko, C. How to Use Humor to Manage Stress. Psychology Today. October 20, 2020. https:// www.psychologytoday.com/intl/blog/play-your-way-sane/202010/how-use-humor-manage -stress?fbclid=IwAR0lQm6E7z8YCwO1Z2HiLd940smFArY6gr9lLgTlhItlopnOO8G8Wg _LvLU.

Enoch, J. The Healing Power of Nature. Metaphysical Source. April 2013. https://www.youtube .com/watch?v=JRRk_MvJ5DI.

Harvard Medical School. In Praise of Gratitude. Harvard Mental Health Letter. June 5, 2019. https:// www.health.harvard.edu/mind-and-mood/in-praise-of-gratitude.

Moore, C. How to Practice Self-Compassion: 8 Techniques and Tips. Positive Psychology.com. October 13, 2020. https://positivepsychology.com/how-to-practice-self-compassion.

Neff, K. *Self-Compassion*. New York, NY: HarperCollins; 2011.

Salmi, L. Redefining the Support Group. TEDxSacramentoSalon. June 16, 2013. https://www.youtube .com/watch?v=htbRPdAjQN4.

Seaward, B. L. Good Vibrations in Troubled Times. WINN. April 10, 2020. https://winnpost.org/2020 /04/10/vibrations.

Seaward, B. L. Laughter in the Time of Coronavirus. Jones & Bartlett Learning Blog. April 30, 2020. https://blogs.jblearning.com/laughter-in-the-time-of-coronavirus.

Seaward, B. L. Words of Wisdom for Adapting and Self-Care During Quarantine from Brian Luke Seaward. April 13, 2020. https://blogs.jblearning.com/words-of-wisdom-from-brian-luke-seaward.

Seaward, B. L., Digital Screen Time: The New Social Addiction. *Alternative and Complementary Therapies* 26(2), April 2020. https://www.brianlukeseaward.com/wp-content/uploads/2020/02/Digital-Screen-Time.pdf.

Seaward, B. L. How to Deal with Threatening Times. WINN.org. September 20, 2019. https://winnpost.org/2019/09/20/how-to-deal-with-threatening-times.

Seaward, B. L. Earth Songs II - Refreshments (The Healing Power of Nature). Deep Blue Seaward Productions. Boulder, CO. April 22, 2019. https://vimeo.com/ondemand/earthsongs.

Tarvin, A. The Skill of Humor. TEDxTamu. June 13, 2017. https://www.youtube.com/watch?v=MdZAMSyn_As.

Winters, S. Self-Care: What It Really Is. TEDxHiltonHeadWomen. December 2018. https://www.ted.com/talks/susannah_winters_self_care_what_it_really_is.

Glossary

A

Acute stress: Distress that is very intense (pounding heartbeat) but short-lived, usually about 15–20 minutes.

Alarm reaction: Considered to be the first stage of the general adaptation syndrome, when stimuli are recognized as a threat and the body goes into fight-or-flight mode.

All-or-none conditioning principle: A concept that says one needs the right intensity, frequency, and duration to produce the benefits of exercise, such as muscle toning, oxygen uptake, and weight loss.

Antioxidants: Compounds that hinder the damaging effect of free radicals on cell membranes, DNA, RNA, and mitochondria.

Artist: Von Oech's second phase of the creative process, wherein the person plays with the raw materials brought back from the explorer's journey.

Auto-immune diseases: Diseases that occur due to an overactive immune system that "attacks" the body. Examples include lupus and rheumatoid arthritis.

B

Bad pain: A sharp pain felt in the joints that persists for a long time, and categories such as sprains, strains, and fractures may require medical attention.

Bioecological influence: Factors that may induce stress in the mind, body, or spirit. Examples might include solar flares, seasonal changes, and weather influences.

Bioflavonoids: Nonnutrients found in foods (fruits and vegetables) that contain antioxidants and seem to provide a means to fight cancer and other illnesses. Bioflavonoids provide the colors in foods.

C

Calculated risk taker: Also called the Type R personality, these people do things to the extreme (e.g., sports). They look at all of their options carefully and then proceed forward.

Cannon, Walter: Renowned Harvard physiologist who coined the term *fight or flight*.

Chakra: The word *chakra* (pronounced SHOCK-ra) is a Sanskrit word meaning spinning wheel. There are thought to be seven primary chakras located from the crown of the head to the base of the spine, each associated with an endocrine gland or region of the body.

Chronic stress: Distress that is not as intense as acute stress, but lasts a long time—days, weeks, months, or even years. Chronic stress is associated with chronic disease.

Circadian rhythms: The biological rhythms in your body based on the internal 24- to 25-hour clock that the body runs on. Sleep cycles and eating cycles are based on circadian rhythms.

Civility: The term, as expressed through social etiquette, refers to the practice of good manners and appropriate behavior.

Codependent personality: Based in the drug and alcohol recovery movement with ties to the enabler, the codependent traits include perfectionism, approval seeking, and victimization, all of which perpetuate the stress process.

Cognitive distortion: In simplest terms, this expression says it all: Making a mountain out of a molehill.

Cortisol: The stress hormone produced in the adrenal glands that is responsible for many metabolic functions related to blood sugar and triglyceride levels in the blood.

Creative blocks: A host of ego-driven attitudes and perceptions that limit one's creative abilities.

Creative problem solving: A term that highlights five steps for creative strategies to solve problems, issues, and concerns. The steps begin with identifying the problem and conclude with an analysis of the solution.

Creative process: There are four phases to the creative process and they must be followed in this order to see the best results: the explorer, the artist, the judge, and the warrior.

Creativity: A very empowering inner resource of an individual to combine imagination with organization, intuition with collaboration, and the right brain's functions with the left brain's skills.

Critical incidence stress management (CISM): Initial treatment of post-traumatic stress disorder with the purpose to significantly reduce the traumatic effects of the incident and prevent further deep-seated PTSD occurrences.

D

Daily life hassles: A term coined by Richard Lazarus to depict the small stressors that tend to add up over the course of a day or two. Unlike chronic stressors that last weeks or months, daily life hassles are little events (like locking your keys in your car) that, when combined with many other little hassles in the course of a day, create a critical mass of stress.

Defense mechanisms: A series of thoughts and behaviors created and used by the ego to protect itself from pain and to promote pleasure. Examples include rationalization, denial, and projection.

Digital dementia: A condition of memory loss experienced by people who indulge in overutilization of digital devices.

Digital toxicity: A neurological stress or burnout from the constant engagement [neuroplasticity] with smartphones and other devices.

Distortion: A dissonance or an imbalance within the layers of energy in the aura which is caused by the unresolved emotional frequencies. Distortion first appears in the aura outside the physical body.

Distress: The unfavorable or negative interpretation of an event to be threatening that promotes continued feelings of fear or anger. Distress is more commonly known simply as stress: a perceived threat (real or imagined) to one's mind, body, spirit, or emotions.

E

Effective coping skills: These include any and all coping skills that help one increase awareness of a problem and/or help resolve an issue. Alcoholism may be a coping technique, but it's not an effective one. Reframing, time management, art therapy, journaling, and creative problem solving are all examples of effective coping skills.

Effective relaxation techniques: The techniques that strive to reduce or eliminate the symptoms of stress and return the body to homeostasis offer the best opportunity to engage the healing process to its fullest potential. Regular physical exercise, walking, and deep breathing are all examples of effective relaxation techniques.

Ego: A term coined by Freud naming the part of the psyche that not only triggers the stress response when threatened, but also defends against all enemies (defense mechanisms) including thoughts and feelings generated from within.

Emotional well-being: The ability to feel and express the entire range of human emotions, but to control them, not be controlled by them.

Energy balance: The difference between calories consumed (meals and snacks eaten) and calories burned (exercise and basal metabolic rate).

Energy psychology: Describes how subtle energy (chakras, meridians, and the human energy field) and subtle anatomy combine with consciousness to either enhance or detract from one's health.

Essential fatty acids: Fatty acids that the body cannot produce and hence that must be consumed from outside sources. Omega-3 (linolenic) acids can be found in flaxseed oil and cold-water fish. Omega-6 (linoleic) acids can be found in various vegetable oils.

Eustress: A sense of happiness or euphoria. Eustress is considered to be "good" stress. Abraham Maslow called this a peak experience. Examples include falling in love or meeting a movie star or sports hero.

Excitotoxins: A name coined by the brain surgeon Russell Blaylock specifically identifying aspartame and MSG as chemical substances that affect brain function because they cross the blood–brain barrier and cause headaches, memory loss, and impaired cognitive function.

Explorer: The first stage of von Oech's creative process, wherein the person goes out and looks for ideas. The explorer is someone who learns to think outside the box.

F

Fear of missing out (FOMO): Anxious behavior associated with an addiction in which the ego needs to be fully engaged with social networking.

Fight-or-flight response: The body's natural response to stress, activated by a perceived threat that cascades from the brain to the adrenal glands for quick movement that allows one to survive. This also includes the Freeze Response (when the fight response fails to engage).

Freeze response: A part of the stress response in which the individual neither fights nor flees, but stays paralyzed like a deer caught in the headlights.

Freud: Considered the pioneer in the emerging field of psychology, laying the groundwork 100 years ago that is still considered to be the cornerstone of psychology. Freud coined the terms ego, defense mechanisms, and many others, forming the basis of contemporary psychology with a strong focus on anxiety (stress).

G

General adaptation syndrome (GAS): A term coined by renowned stress researcher Hans Selye, describing the three phases in which stress takes its toll on the body.

Genetically modified organisms (GMOs): Food that has been genetically altered by splicing DNA from other species (e.g., the gene of a flounder fish into tomatoes). GMOs are related to many food allergies and are considered to be a stress to the body.

Good pain: A dull pain felt when the muscles are sore (comes from the lack of use) and typically disappears within hours to a day or so.

Good vibes: *The generation or recognition of* positive feelings that come from people, places, and happenings.

H

Hardy personality: Three traits comprise the hardy personality: challenge, control, and commitment, all of which combine to help this type of person to overcome any adversity.

Helpless–hopeless: Personality best-described by individuals who consider self-esteem crucial and lack personal resources that help cope with problems.

Holistic medicine: A healing approach that honors the integration, balance, and harmony of mind, body, spirit, and emotions to promote inner peace. Every technique used in stress management is considered to support the concept of holistic medicine. Also called alternative medicine.

Homeostasis: A term coined by Claude Bernard to represent the body's condition at complete rest.

Human energy field: Also known as the electromagnetic field around an object and as a colorful aura. The human energy field is thought to be composed of layers of consciousness that surround and permeate the physical body.

I

Immune system–related disorders: Health issues that arise from either an underactive (e.g., colds, flus, cancer) or overactive immune system (e.g., lupus, rheumatoid arthritis), each of which is affected by stress.

Inflammation: The body's response to an injury or stress.

Infradian rhythms: Biological rhythms that occur more than 24-hour period (e.g., the menses).

Insomnia: Disturbance in the quality and quantity of sleep presented as poor-quality sleep or abnormal wakefulness.

J

Judge: Von Oech identifies the role of the judge as the third stage of the creative process, but one people typically place first, thus compromising the entire process.

Jung, Carl: Twentieth-century physician who, under the initial tutelage of Sigmund Freud, forged a new premise of psychology honoring the importance of the human spirit, becoming the second greatest influence in the field of psychology.

L

Lazarus, Richard: A renowned psychologist who coined the term *daily life hassles.*

Life change units (LCUs): A unit of stress as determined by the number of stressful life episodes one has had at a certain point in one's life.

Lipids: Fats that are liquid at room temperature and are prone to becoming rancid when they are subjected to heat and light.

M

Mechanistic model: A theory that suggests that just as the universe operates like a big grandfather clock, so, too, does the body. This model denies the existence of the human spirit.

Mental well-being: The ability to gather, process, recall, and communicate information. Also called intellectual well-being.

Meridians: First described by Chinese medicine, a meridian is a river of energy that runs through the body. Humans have 12 major meridians, and each meridian has a pulse. Blocks or congestion at any point in the meridian are typically addressed using an acupuncture needle (or shiatsu).

Microbiome: The multitude of intestinal flora of bacteria needed for a healthy body.

Myers-Briggs Type Indicator: A self-report inventory designed to identify a person's personality type, strengths, and preferences.

N

Nervous system–related disorders: Stress-related physical symptoms initiated by an overactive nervous system. These include, but are not limited to, headaches, irritable bowel syndrome, and hypertension.

Neuropeptides: Chemical compounds (perhaps as many as 600) not only secreted in the brain, but also now known to be manufactured by cells throughout the body. These chemicals have the unique ability to communicate to each other in a fashion not yet understood by Western science.

Neustress: Any kind of information or sensory stimulus that is perceived as unimportant or nonconsequential.

O

Organic foods: Foods that are certified to be grown in clean soil with no use of herbicides, pesticides, fungicides, or synthetic fertilizers.

P

Physical exercise: Either aerobic (with the use of oxygen) or anaerobic (without the use of oxygen) work that develops the cardiovascular and musculoskeletal systems, respectively.

Physical well-being: The ability to ensure health, avoid preventable diseases and conditions, and optimal functioning of the body's physiological systems such as cardiovascular, endocrine, reproductive, immune.

Pilates: A type of exercise developed by Joseph Pilates early in the 20th century to strengthen the core muscles of the body's frame and may indeed help chronic pain. It was mainly used by dancers and athletes for both prevention and rehabilitation of athletic injuries.

Positive affirmations: The ability to give oneself positive feedback in the midst of a bad situation so that one does not get sucked into the vortex of negativity. Positive affirmation is not a denial of a bad situation; rather, it is the ability to rise above it.

Posttraumatic stress disorder (PTSD): An emotional disorder that can occur in people who have experienced a traumatic event.

Psychic equilibrium: The ability of overcoming stress by redirecting negative thoughts in a positive direction to achieve success.

Psychic tension: Stress built up within an individual's mind due to the prolonged accumulation of negative or fear-based thoughts, attitudes, beliefs, and perceptions. According to Carl Jung, it is the constant mental chatter of the ego.

Psychointrapersonal influences: Stressors that originate in the mind, either real or imagined. These are usually the result of ego-driven issues.

R

Reframing: The ability to change one's perception from a negative to a more positive approach. Some would add it includes seeing the benefit from a bad situation.

Resiliency: Ability of an individual to handle difficulties and recover with self-esteem.

S

Seasonal affective disorder (SAD): A condition brought on by the lack of direct sunlight (usually during the winter months) that affects one's production of melatonin and hence serotonin, resulting in symptoms of depression.

Self-care: Taking intentional time to nurture one's physical, mental, emotional, and spiritual health on a daily basis.

Self-compassion: The ability to turn understanding, acceptance, and love inward.

Self-healing: The body's unique ability to restore a sense of homeostasis when not interrupted by stress, poor nutrition, and the like. An example is a fever, which is the body's way to kill off invading microbes.

Sleep hygiene: A term used to describe the environment one sleeps in with regard to room temperature, darkness, silence (or noise), disrupting pets, and bedding. It also takes into account circumstances affecting sleep patterns such as caffeine intake and irregular shift work. Poor sleep hygiene is thought to be associated with poor sleep.

Social influences: Stressors generated from external sources such as traffic, urban sprawl, and ex-spouses.

Social Readjustment Rating Scale (SRRS): A scale developed by Holmes and Rahe using life-change units to determine one's level of stress.

Spiritual well-being: The maturation of higher consciousness as developed through the integration of three facets: relationships, values, and a meaningful purpose in one's life. A fourth facet is the acknowledgment of the divine mystery of life.

Stage of exhaustion: The third stage of Selye's general adaptation syndrome, in which one or more organs

targeted by excessive neural or hormonal activity goes into dysfunction.

Stage of resistance: The second stage of Selye's general adaptation syndrome, in which the body and all its organs try to return to homeostasis. If the stress persists, this may not be possible and the third stage begins.

Stress reaction: Any strategy that leads one back in the direction of homeostasis. Holistic stress management includes using both effective coping skills (mind) and relaxation techniques (body) to address both causes and symptoms, respectively.

Stress response: The same as the fight-or-flight response.

Stressor: Any issue, concern, or problem that is perceived to be a threat to one's mind, body, spirit, or emotions.

Stress-prone personality: A collection of personalities that promote stress rather than diminish it. These include the Type A personality, the codependent personality, and the helpless-hopeless personality.

Stress-resistant personality: These are personality traits that allow a person to cope well with stress, giving the appearance that they are resistant to crisis. These include the hardy personality, the survivor personality, and the sensation seeker, also known as Type R.

Subtle anatomy: Also called energy anatomy, subtle anatomy is composed of the human energy field (aura), the chakra system, and the meridian system of energetic pathways that supply energy (also known as chi or prana) to the organs and physiological systems with which they connect.

Survivor personality: A collection of personality traits that combine to enhance one's ability to survive stressful events.

T

Technostress: A term coined to focus on the stress induced by the proliferation of technology from smartphones to upgrades, downloads to laptops.

Tend and befriend: A theory presented by Shelly Taylor which states that women who experience stress don't necessarily run or fight, but rather turn to friends to cope with unpleasant events and circumstances.

The power of the mind: The collective spirit of both conscious and unconscious minds to work in unison.

Toxic thoughts: Thoughts and perceptions created by the mind (specifically, the ego) that chip away at one's self-esteem. Toxic thoughts perpetuate stress.

Trans-fatty acids: Form of saturated fat and tend to destroy cell membranes by blocking the gates that allow nutrients to go in and waste products to leave.

Type A personality: Initially called the worry sickness, Type A behavior is now regarded as the aggressive-based personality, with traits that are associated with coronary heart disease.

U

Ultradian rhythms: Biological rhythms that occur many times in a 24-hour period (e.g., hunger pangs).

W

Warrior: This is the fourth stage of von Oech's creative process, wherein the warrior takes the idea to the street (marketing and implementation).

Well-being: The integration, balance, and harmony of one's mind, body, spirit, and emotions. More generally, well-being is just feeling well. Mental, physical, emotional, and spiritual well-being are four types of well-being.

Y

Yerkes-Dodson principle: A concept that suggests that some stress (excitement or stimuli) is good to a point, then it becomes bad. Up to a point this enhances one's performance, past that point, it diminishes it. This "point" is different for everyone.

Index

Note: Page numbers followed by 'f' indicate materials in figures.